The Mystery of Faith

By

Vernon Ball

Bonnie,

You are such a great addition to our family. Your love, support and persistance have contributed so much in getting this book into print. It is my prayer that you are blessed by this work as you have been a blessing. As you continue your journey of faith may the Lord grant you many victories.

Because of Jesus

Vernon

Acknowledgements:

T he Bible declares that "we are His workmanship" and as such, I must credit the Lord for everything that I have and will become. Furthermore, I confess that it was the Holy Spirit's leading that has prompted me to put this book together. It was His revelation that was so inspiring and encouraging to me as I learned these principles before I could share them. Without Him, I would have nothing of value to say.

I know that my parents, who passed a number of years ago, were also instrumental in establishing my value system. I thank the Lord for their correction as well as their love and example.

A call to preach is a call to prepare. I owe a debt to all of those who have sacrificed and worked to establish strong Biblical educational schools. A school won't make you a preacher, but if you are called of God, it will make you a better one. I thank the Lord for making a way for me to attend Clear Creek Baptist Bible College.

The strongest human support a man can have is a supportive wife. I have been abundantly blessed with my wife, Darla for her support and sacrifice so that I could attend school with a family and later serve in small church settings, enduring hardship that we might serve the Lord there.

Dr. Bill Whittegar has been a strong supporter of preachers since I have known him. As president of Clear Creek Baptist College, he invited me to speak at chapel while I was writing this book and encouraged me to finish, which took several years. He was an obvious choice to review this work and contributed many helpful suggestions.

I must confess that the idea of writing a book was daunting, but the Lord brought Laura Werling to help edit this work. Her untold hours of service have not gone unnoticed or unappreciated. May the Lord richly reward you, Laura.

My family has been a team of encouragement and support. Their patience and input has been quite valuable. I want to especially thank my son, Daniel, for his many recommendations and his part in editing this work into its final form.

Finally, I offer a word of thanks to all of the individuals who have listened to me, given valuable input, and have prayed for me and for this work. May the Lord be magnified. You will not lose your reward.

Preface

I have no greater joy than to hear that my children walk in truth.

–John 3:4

It is the burden of my heart to see Christians victorious in their faith in the Lord Jesus. The world yearns to see God work in the lives of the believer. If they do not see it, they will label us hypocrites, but if and when they do see Him work in the life of the believer, they will want to know how God can work in their own lives. People are hurting everywhere and are searching for answers. We know that Jesus is the answer, and faith in Him is the only way to please Him. My prayer is that you will incorporate these principles of faith in your life and that you will become that light unto others so that they too will choose Jesus. This is the greatest evangelistic program the church has.

While it is true that faith is a mystery, it should not be a mystery to Christians. The Bible is replete with examples of individuals who had no training, no experience and no model of faith from which to learn; yet, they became heroes of faith. Hebrews 11 provides many such examples.

The title of this book is taken from 1 Timothy 3:9 "Holding the mystery of the faith in a pure conscience." It is one of the twelve specific mysteries mentioned in the New Testament.[1] A mystery

---

[1] The general concept of mystery is mentioned 22 times in the New Testament, but some instances reference the same subject. The 10 other mysteries include the kingdom of God, Israel's blindness, the gospel, the resurrection, God's will, the church, iniquity, godliness, Christ in you, and Babylon.

is a subject with hidden truths that are not readily apparent. It is God's intention to reveal these mysteries to His children, but they are not understood with the natural mind. [2] Unlocking the mystery of faith requires the new birth, study of the scriptures, and the Holy Spirit who is our teacher. God intends to unlock these mysteries and wants for us to know them, but they will remain a mystery until we approach them God's way.

This book is a product of my study and practice of the principles of walking by faith for over 44 years of ministry. When I reference the word faith, it is understood that I am not speaking of faith as some quality or substance that I possess and that causes God to respond. In fact, it is just the opposite. *Faith* is the principle of trusting or relying on Jesus, the one who will develop you to respond to Him. He is the author and the finisher of our faith, so it is initiated and brought to completion by Him. [3] Our part of believing is sandwiched between these two points. Chapter four expands this principle more.

This book is intended to be a reference guide or manual to assist the believer in his journey through life as he prepares for eternity. It should be carefully and prayerfully read and studied repeatedly. You will no doubt understand some concepts without difficulty while others may require more time and experience. I challenge you to conduct a thorough investigation in your understanding of this mystery of faith.

---

[2] But the natural man receiveth not the things of the Spirit of God: for they are foolish-ness unto him: neither can he know them, because they are spiritually discerned (1Co 2:14).

[3] Hebrews 12:2

Table of Contents

Chapter 1

Misconceptions of Faith

When I was 26, I drove a 1964 Mercury Comet. Two months before I started my freshman year at Clear Creek Baptist Bible College, it had 99,000 miles. The body was dimpled with hail damage, which, at a certain angle, resembled the surface of a golf ball, and it vibrated fiercely when I went over 60 mph. I knew it wouldn't see me through until graduation, but I couldn't afford payments on a used car, not while I was in school. My first semester was starting soon, and I was out of ideas. I prayed about it, but I didn't sense any direction.

One morning I was walking through a shopping center and noticed that there was a drawing for a new car. As I gazed at the shinny white compact, I knew, without any question, that this was how God was going to provide for me. I promptly filled out my information slip and dropped it into the box. I was confident I would win. I even thanked the Lord for my new car before leaving the shopping center. I was so excited. I couldn't wait for the day of the drawing. The closer it came, the more anxious I became, and I wondered how I would be notified. Finally, the day of the drawing arrived. Morning came and went, but I didn't hear anything, and I wondered if maybe they had trouble contacting me. Afternoon came, then evening and then two and three days. Still no one called. About a week after the drawing, it finally sunk in that I did not win the car, and I wondered what had happened. I was so sure that the car was mine, and I couldn't understand why God didn't let me win.

It is not uncommon for Christians –especially new Christians–
to be naïve about faith or be tossed about with every wind of
doctrine. That doctrine of faith may range from a confused, miscon-
strued belief system to an accurate and beautiful portrait of Christ.
According to Hebrews 6:1, faith is foundational to the Christian life.
It is a basic doctrine on which we build our relationship with Jesus,
conduct our affairs, and make choices. It is therefore essential that
we first address some of the misconceptions about faith, which warp
our understanding of how it functions in our lives.

Faith is not quantifiable

One misconception of faith is that individuals must have *enough*
faith to be successful in some endeavor; however, just the opposite
is taught in the Bible.[4] A mustard seed is extremely small, but even
this amount of faith is adequate for God's purposes. When the object
of our faith is the Lord, great things are the result.

Even for a mustard seed, faith works mightily.[5,6] Therefore, what
prevents faith from working in our lives is not the amount of faith
we have but where we have placed our faith. Faith in anything other
than Jesus is unbelief.

This principle is evident as I reflect on my own experience. I
didn't win a new car, but my '64 Comet lasted all through school.
Around the time I graduated, it had 168,000 miles and was still running. That year, I traded it for a station wagon that was more fitting
to my growing family. It is clear that my faith had been in the shinny
new car and not in the Lord. God provided me the transportation that
I needed, but he did it His way.

---

[4] And Jesus said unto them, Because of your unbelief: for verily I say unto you, If ye
have faith as a grain of mustard seed, ye shall say unto this mountain, Remove hence to
yonder place; and it shall remove; and nothing shall be impossible unto you. Matthew
17:20

[5] It is like a grain of mustard seed, which a man took, and cast into his garden; and it
grew, and waxed a great tree; and the fowls of the air lodged in the branches of it Lu
13:19.

[6] And the Lord said, If ye had faith as a grain of mustard seed, ye might say unto this syc-
amore tree, be thou plucked up by the root, and be thou planted in the sea; and it should
obey you Lu 17:6.

We make similar errors when we qualify the outcome of our circumstances (e.g. I am trusting Jesus to do something for me), forge Jesus' name (e.g. adding His name to a prayer that is not Spirit-led), trust another person or entity (e.g. crossing a bridge that appears safe but isn't) or any other such qualified response that is not a full surrender to Jesus. If you trust Him, the results are up to Him and Him alone.

Faith is not a substance

Although Hebrews 11:1 says that "faith is the substance of things hoped for, the evidence of things not yet seen," this verse is not a definition of faith. It is not a material substance that can be mined like gold and spent when needed. Instead, faith is a description of the assurance and confidence that a Christian has when responding to what God has revealed. Although we cannot accumulate faith, we can grow in it, and we do so by exercising the faith we already have. It is similar to crawling, which leads to walking, which leads to running.

Not only must faith be exercised, it also needs to be nourished. Faith is nourished with proper understanding of who Jesus is and His will. This is discovered through study of the Bible, prayer, and a personal relationship with the Lord. It is important to not only know of Jesus but to know Him intimately. This will bring about the stability of a sure foundation and a hope of what is yet ahead.

Faith is not magical

We often perceive that faith is some magical, far-out concept that works a lot like chance, that the inner workings of faith are unknowable. Though faith is a mystery to the worldly mind, it can be understood in the Spirit, and moreover it works by a given set of principles.[7] These principles of faith are devoid of the use of the efforts of the will of man and the use of powers of darkness. They are always in agreement with the Word of God.

---

[7] I expand more on these principles in Chapter 4: The Operation of Faith.

One kind of faith

Then there are those who suggest that there are different kinds of faith. These individuals would have you to believe that there is "saving faith," "justifying faith," or "enduring faith." However, these terms all refer to the same concept, which can be defined as trust, reliance, or dependence upon. The issue is not the type of faith but the object or focus of faith.

It is worth asking: in whom are you trusting? If you trust a doctor, he makes the diagnosis and prescribes the appropriate course of healing. If you trust an investment banker, he does the investing. If you trust a mechanic, he does the repair. If you trust Jesus to deliver you from this present evil age, He directs the way as your Lord. He is not a genie to grant you wishes, a waiter to satisfy your hunger or a host to maintain your comfort. He is your Lord to direct and redirect you so that He may deliver you to the Father, spotless and blameless, in love.[8]

Everyone lives by faith, but not everyone lives by faith in Jesus as Lord. In fact, it is impossible to live in this world without faith. You must trust someone or something. The issue is not whether you have faith but where that faith is applied. Ultimately, it comes down to either trusting in Jesus or the world. The world includes your own judgment, another person or thing. Before you can choose Jesus, you need to discover that you are not trustworthy and that He is. Only then will you be willing to rely on Him instead of yourself, and only then will your faith in Him be activated to cause change.

Faith is seeing!

Faith is a mystery[9] until it is revealed to us by the Holy Spirit. Some have taken the liberty to explain it in purely physical terms and have, in the process, utterly confused the teaching or doctrine, which explains common expressions, such as *blind faith*. Just because you do not control it does not necessitate blindness. Consider the expression *seeing is believing*. The truth is just the opposite: *believing is seeing*.

---

[8] Ephesians 1:4

[9] Holding the mystery of the faith in a pure conscience. I Timothy 3:9

Also consider the 11th chapter of Hebrews, verses 3-13. Able, Enoch, Noah, Abraham and Sarah all received a promise from God, and having seen these promises, they were persuaded by them and embraced them. Though they didn't actually see the promises with their eyes, they saw them in the same way we see an idea. The problem is that you can't see the invisible – but they did.

Faith does not cause us to blindly step into the unknown but to step into what is known or revealed spiritually. If there is no spiritual revealing, we cannot walk by faith. We are not expected to out guess God and anticipate where He may want us, nor are we to second guess God and figure out His will before it is revealed. Untold tragedy awaits those who carelessly proceed without God's revelation.

One word of caution: If you reject Jesus as your way, your truth and your life, you will turn to flawed means and methods of finding your way. A common definition of insanity is trying the same thing repeatedly, expecting a different result with each attempt. It doesn't take long to discover that we are flawed and cannot meet the standard of perfection. At this point, a decision has to be made: do you trust someone or something else or do you continue doing the best you can, expecting a different result? No matter what you choose to trust in –yourself or someone else– everything *in this world* is flawed and will fail you.[10]

---

[10] The choice of who or what you serve is clarified in *Ro 6:16 Know ye not, that to whom ye yield yourselves servants to obey, his servants ye are to whom ye obey; whether of sin unto death, or of obedience unto righteousness.*

Chapter 2

The Necessity of Faith

The just shall live by faith.
– Habakkuk 2:4, Romans 1:17, Galatians 3:11, Hebrews 10:38

I was attending a Christian conference in Maryland several years ago, and the speaker was talking about making decisions. I was stunned to hear that 95% of all decisions, both small and great, are made emotionally. He went on to say that the advertisement industry is very aware of this and makes millions of dollars by using the emotions to enhance sales. Astute politicians also capitalize on this information and entice votes by promising things that the populace wants, rather than what they need. Careers are chosen by our desire to succeed. Husbands and wives are chosen by how they make us feel, and employees are hired for what they can do, rather than who they are. The truth is that we are enslaved by our emotions and desires. The Bible speaks to this in Romans 6:16 "Know ye not, that to whom ye yield yourselves servants to obey, his servants ye are to whom ye obey; whether of sin unto death, or of obedience unto righteousness." We follow our lower nature of sin and therefore make decisions that hurt others and us. God's plan to deliver man from this present evil age requires him to live by faith in the Lord and not to rely on, or even to trust his unnatural instincts. Faith in God was the natural way for man to live and is still necessary for us to live victoriously today. We know this because it is required by scripture, because we were designed to live by faith and because God is in Control of the events of our lives.

It is required by Scripture

It is not uncommon to find a scripture passage recurring in one, or even two books, but *"the just shall live by faith"* can be found in four different places throughout the Bible.[11] Perhaps this is because this principle is foundational in God's plan for mankind. It is a basic requirement in our relationship to God. If we fail to establish this principle at the beginning of our Christian walk, we will certainly run into many barriers and frustrations, and we will not have a vital personal relationship with God. It does not matter how hard you try, how much you do, or how much you sacrifice. This is God's requirement for us, and we will not be justified without it.

The only means of pleasing God is that you live by faith in Him.[12] This means that no work will be accepted that is not a faith work. No ministry will be pleasing to Him that He is not in charge of. Nothing will please Him that is not of faith. If you could do it without Him, you would not trust Him to do it. If you started it, you are in charge; however, if it is impossible for you, and you don't know how to proceed, you are ready to trust Him by faith. If it doesn't require His wisdom and power, it probably doesn't require faith either and would not please God.

Not only is it required by scripture and is the only way to please God, but all other ways are rejected. Romans 14:23b concludes that "whatsoever is not of faith is sin." Quite often we hear Christians justify themselves by what they do or by what they don't do. God is not impressed with our efforts, as the Bible has concluded, "all have sinned and come short of His Glory."[13]

This is the point where the natural man stumbles. He thinks that there must be some other way.[14] The way of faith is foreign and unnatural to him. It makes him uncomfortable. It does not make sense that God would forgive sin and count a man righteous

---

[11] Habakkuk 2:4, Romans 1:17, Galatians 3:11, and Hebrews 10:38.

[12] Hebrews 11:6a says, *"without faith [in Jesus] it is impossible to please [God]. . ."*

[13] Jeremiah 17:9, Isaiah 53:6, Romans 3:9-10, 23, Galatians 3:22

[14] Proverbs 14:12

by simply placing one's faith in Jesus. The problem lies in the fact that man cannot accept his total sinfulness and his belief that his goodness outweighs his sinfulness.

This idea that our good outweighs our sinfulness is really the unreasonable position. Consider the hypothetical situation of someone who had lived his life perfectly for 50 years and for whatever reason committed a murder. If he were to stand before the court of the land and was found guilty, the law would require him to pay for his one sin. The argument of 50 years of perfect living wouldn't offset the law's requirement. If we, as mere imperfect humans, require the satisfaction of the law, why would we think that God would use a lesser standard? The law demands justice, and Jesus accepted that judgment on our part on the cross.

Although Jesus paid the penalty of sin, that payment is on the condition of belief. Since justice has been satisfied, no one goes to hell simply as a result of his sin[15] but for his refusal to believe in the Lord Jesus. The reason God requires belief is because it forces us to face our guilt and humble ourselves before Him. God has removed all of the obstacles that are in our way. The only barrier to receiving God's new life is choice.

Not only is faith required to receive this new life, but it is also required to live this life. Living by faith in the Lord Jesus is the most exciting and fulfilling experience that I can imagine. As the relationship grows, there is an ever-widening circle of understanding and fulfillment. Life makes more sense and becomes more rewarding. Values change and you venture into experiences with a peace that passes understanding. Even when you make mistakes, there is forgiveness and hope. God's plan for you is that you grow in faith all the way to maturity. Consider Romans 8:14. "For as many as are led by the Spirit of God, they are the Sons of God." Literally, it means that those who are continually being led by the Spirit of God are the mature Sons of God. This is what a mature Christian acts like. He is continually being led by faith in Jesus as Lord of his life.

---

[15] John 3:16-18

We were designed to live by faith

What does it mean to live by faith in Him? This is a valid question and must be understood in the light of what God intended when He set the order of His creation. Faith in God was required from the very first instruction that God gave Adam when he was directed not to eat of the tree in the midst of the Garden of Eden. God fully understood the probability that man would not make the right choices because His image, likeness and dominion were not yet completed in him. Further, man was unaware of Satan, his plans and power. Equally important, God knew what was yet to be revealed to complete man and make him a child of God. Even though man was created by God, he does not become a child of God until he is *born again* or *born of the Spirit*. That is what Jesus was talking about in John 3:5: "Except a man be born of water and of the Spirit, he cannot enter into the kingdom of God." You must be born physically (the water birth) and spiritually (the spiritual birth) in order to be completed. This is confirmed in II Corinthians 5:17: "Therefore, if any man be in Christ he is a new creature (literally a new creation): old things are passed away; behold all things are become new."

This is God's chosen relationship with man, that man is to place himself in the position of dependence and trust upon the Lord. The Lord then takes full responsibility for what the individual is, does and becomes. It does not happen because a person walks down an aisle, says certain words, feels a certain way, hears a certain preacher, is in extreme circumstances, has Christian parents, or any other such thing. It happens upon only one condition, that the person places their *faith* in Jesus as Lord of life.[16]

Some might think God will save them if they submit to some ritual and have a sincere desire to go to heaven. This is not entirely true and will not necessarily produce a new birth. What is needed is for that individual to get aligned with Jesus in such a way that he is dependent upon Him for health, wealth, and will. If you are dependent upon the Lord, you are not dependent on outside sources or even yourself. It means that your outcome is reliant upon Him and no other.

---

[16] Here faith is differentiated from hope. Hope in the lord is an entirely different issue.

Another way to understand what it means to place your faith in Jesus is to become intimate with Him, meaning that you must know Him in such a way that you can trust Him without reservation. No one would commit their weight to an old frayed rope, and no one will trust Jesus unless they know how loving and powerful He is. A person might believe that they have faith in Jesus just because they have asked Him into their heart. Though such a person may be born again, it is not because of their invitation but because of their surrender. I do not want to get hung up on the words that one uses to become saved. That is not especially important because God looks at the heart and not at the words. The issue is not whether you say it correctly but whether you believe it correctly.[17] There is only one way that Jesus will come into a life, and that is if a person accepts Him as Lord of life. Consider the young girl who was afraid that she had become pregnant because she had kissed a boy for the first time. She thought that was the kind of intimacy that would produce a new life. You cannot anymore be born again without this kind of intimacy than you can become pregnant by kissing.

To place your faith in Jesus also includes an element of trust. Trust is not equal to faith but is contained within faith. Trust is not spoken about a lot in today's religious circles, but it is a critical element in a right relationship with the Lord. To trust someone is to rely upon, to count on or to place confidence in another. In faith, trust is placed in Jesus. It means that you have placed Him in charge and accept the results at His hand. It is impossible to do this if you have never met Him or do not believe that He has your best interests at heart. If your perspective of Jesus is that He is full of the same faults as others, you would be foolhardy to trust Him. Trust is a developed relationship. The more you know Him the more you trust Him. We trust Him for a few safe things and grow into a more complete trust. Only those who know Him well trust him extensively.

There are a number of obstacles to trust in today's world. One such obstacle is fear. It rises in our hearts because we know that to trust may result in suffering and loss. When this distrust is carried over into our spiritual lives, it conflicts with the Holy Spirit and robs

---

[17] And they said, believe on the Lord Jesus Christ, and thou shalt be saved, and thy house. Acts 16:31.

us of our joy and peace. It is much like the young couple who lived several miles from town during the settlement of the American west. One day, the man's wife became gravely ill, so he went out in the snow and ice to get a doctor from the nearest town. On his way, he came to a river and found that it had frozen over. As he stood there at the edge of the river, he wondered how thick the ice was. He had seen the river flowing just a few days before and thought that if the ice broke, he might drown and no one would know to get the doctor for his wife. He finally decided that he had a better chance of making it to the other side if he crawled on his stomach. Slowly, he began to edge across the river. As he got about halfway, he heard a series of loud thumps rumbling in his direction. When it got closer, he saw it was a large lumber wagon, and it began to cross the river. He watched in horror as this wagon began to make its way to the other side but was much relieved as it rumbled over the ice past him. After it had disappeared into the woods, he thought about how foolish he must have looked to the driver, laying there on the ice. He had been terrified that it might break; yet, it could hold up the wagon of lumber and team of horses. How much like this young man we are when we fear that the Lord will not bear us up under our light load of afflictions. If only we would trust Him.

Another barrier to trust is our self-interests. If you were to give a child a quarter of a dollar, he would naturally close his hand over the quarter. The problem now is that a closed fist is not open to receive any more blessings. If you ask the child to hold out his fist and open his hand, he will be reluctant to do it because of this sin nature. If he knows you well enough to trust you, he may open his hand because of his trust in you. This is what God does with us in requiring us to place our faith in Him. When we know that we can trust Him, we will begin to operate on the standard of trust in the Lord instead of trusting in ourselves. Once we experience the results of trusting God instead of our old sin nature, we begin to see the possibilities of what God wants to do in our lives, and we begin to exchange our methods for His, which makes an eternal change in us.

A third barrier to trusting Christ is the belief that more understanding about faith will help us to trust Him more; however, knowledge and understanding do not aid us in trusting the Lord. In fact, the more we know intellectually —without experience— the more we are apt to trust our own understanding, rather than Him. Faith is known more experientially than it is intellectually. For example, you can study what it is like to fly. You can learn all there is to know about how air moves over a wing, the effects of altitude, weight/lift ratios, temperature and weather changes, or the strengths of different materials; however, you still will not really know what it is to fly. Yet a person can understand flight quite well after flying just one time. So it is with faith. To understand it, you must experience it.

We were designed to live by faith, and that is why faith is so important. This design includes the exultation of fulfillment, capacity to receive God's blessings, transformation into all that we can be and understanding of the spiritual realm. We are designed with eternity in mind and not for this world only. Our faith experiences build our confidence in God as we discover His control over the events of life and how the spiritual world coexists with, and is a part of this physical life.

God is in control

We need to discover that He is in charge and that nothing can touch us without His permission. If your concept of God is that he is just waiting for you to mess up so he can punish you for your failure, you do not know Him. It is vital to understand that all things work together for good to them who love God, to them who are called according to His purpose.[18] Even our failures and our mistakes teach us the value of placing our faith in God. Our successes bring encouragement and give us confidence to continue walking by faith.

God is in control of events. For the Christian there is no such thing as a chance happening. Keep in mind, however, that even though God is in control of the ultimate outcome, he does not interfere with man's free choice. Though we may be targeted for evil, God is able to use that effort and turn it to our good. Joseph was sold into slavery by his brothers. He was wrongly accused, innocently jailed and forgotten for years. God used all of these events to prepare him to become the vice regent over Egypt, and he later declared to

---

[18] Romans 8:28

his brothers that, even though they meant it for evil, God meant it for good. Though the road may not be easy, it is always good.

God has a plan for our lives. Even though this plan may not encompass specific details, such as the profession we choose or what works we may do, he intends for us to be delivered from the bondage of sin. I doubt that He has a quota for so many carpenters, or businessmen or even preachers. I rather think that He is great enough to use us in any field of endeavor we may choose. The urgent need for us is that sin loses its grip on our lives and that we come to trust that God is always working to our benefit in all ways. His plan for us is our ultimate total deliverance from sin.[19]

The universe belongs to Him. The Bible declares that the whole world belongs to Him and that all creation is made by Him and for Him.[20] God is the owner of all things, and if that isn't enough, he can create more. He has no shortages.[21]

The scriptures are clear that faith in the Lord is not an option. Not only is it required that we live by faith, but it is impossible to please God any other way. The Bible has extensive scripture on faith, and its theme runs from Genesis through the book of Revelation.

---

[19] *In the body of his flesh through death, to present you holy and unblamable and unreproveable in his sight. Colossians 1:22*

[20] Colossions1:16

[21] For of Him, and through Him, and to Him, are all things: to whom be glory forever. Romans 11:36

Chapter 3

The Objective of Faith

For therein is the righteousness of God revealed from faith to faith.

– Romans 1:17

How does faith in Christ fit into the plan of God for man? Man was first made a living soul.[22] He then sinned and was alienated from God, so God confronted him about it so that man might be rescued from sin and its penalty, restored to fellowship and returned to his position of being transformed into the image of God. Until sin is confronted, there will be no rejection of it. Faith in Christ is the response of the believer of trust and reliance on God for life. Faith in Christ is in response to seeing one's true condition and surrendering the management of that life back to God. Once Faith in Christ as Lord is established, He will proceed to finish the transformation of man into His image. The Lord is and always has been for you, and it is His desire to confirm you as His child.

God's Diagram for man

Why did God make man? The key verse that unlocks the door to this question is found in Genesis 1:26.

And God said, Let us make man in our image, after our likeness: and let them have dominion over the fish of the sea, and over the fowl of the air, and over the cattle, and over all the earth,

---

[22] 1 Colossians 15:45

and over every creeping thing that creepeth upon the earth.

Simply put, God made man for the purpose of fellowshipping with him. This verse tells us that there are at least three characteristics that are essential for fellowship with God: man must be made in the same image, in the same likeness, and with the same capacity to rule rightly. Let's look at each of these more closely.

While it is true that man was made in the image of God, He doesn't have a physical form. He is Spirit.[23] What this means is that man was made in the similitude of God, and each part represents a truth about Him. For example, when the hands make something, it represents God's creative abilities. Man's voice represents God's communicative abilities. A man's mind is reminiscent of God's omniscience, God's all-knowledge. The strength of man is illustrative of God's omnipotence, God's power. Even man's eyes and his ability to perceive amazing detail from a distance tells us of God's perception or ability to see into our heart and soul and spirit. Everything about a man should tell us something about our Creator. Perhaps one of the reasons that we are commanded to not murder another man is that we would be damaging the image of God. James 3:9 says that man was made in the similitude of God. Man is the pinnacle of God's creation. No life form ever made exceeds man because he is the picture of God.

Secondly, man was made in the likeness of God. That means that he was created and made with a disposition, character and value system. When completed, he will be like God in his decision making, in his values, in his work and in his ethics. He has a personality and finds joy and humor as well as sadness and pain in varying situations. Every person is unique and special. In all of God's creation, only humanity is offered the opportunity to become a child of God. Perhaps that is part of why He loves us so much. Man is able to make independent thoughts and decisions based upon who he is and receive and communicate those thoughts with others. He has a highly developed sense of intellect with the capacity to make decisions. He is a free moral agent and carries the responsibility for his choices.

---

[23] God is a spirit and they that worship Him, must worship Hi in Spirit and in truth. John 4:24

God's plan for man is not to make him a robot that copies actions in an assembly line fashion but to be a free moral agent that chooses the same things that God chooses, one who can respond to God in the same fashion that Christ does.

In this life we are "under construction" and are not completed until God's plan for man is completed. And just what is that plan? "That He might present it to Himself a glorious church, not having spot, or wrinkle, or any such thing; but that it should be holy and without blemish."[24] This can only be accomplished when we are separated from our sin and born again.[25], [26], [27] Not only is God's plan to separate us from sin, but also to then preserve and deliver us without spot or wrinkle, fully completed forever. God's deliverance is through faith in Jesus as Lord of Life.

Thirdly, man was made with the capacity to *rule*. God governs the entirety of creation. It is His choice that man develops his dominion over the physical creation, which is temporal. This limited authority in our lives will prepare us for reigning with Christ in eternity. One of the lessons that must be learned is how to live under authority, and we must learn this before we can live in authority. God uses the physical realm to teach us the spiritual realities.

There are seven authority relationships that God has established in this life that work together to prepare us for that reign:

Marital Authority	Husband/Wife
Parental Authority	Parents/Children
Educational Authority	Teacher/Student
Administrative Authority	Employer/Employee
Governmental Authority	Government/Citizen
Ecclesiastical Authority	Church/Member
Scriptural Authority	Bible/Person

---

[24] Ephesians 5:27

[25] Who gave Himself for our sins, that He might deliver us from this present evil world, according to the will of God and our Father. Galatians 1:4

[26] And the Lord shall deliver me from every evil work, and will preserve me unto his heavenly kingdom: to whom be glory forever and ever. 2 Timothy 4:18

[27] And ye are complete in Him, which is the head of all principality and power. Colossians 2:10

In Chapter 10, we will examine the ideas of authority and rule in more detail. For now, however, just note that we are under authority from the time of birth. As we mature, we learn how this principle works, and we begin to grow in our understanding of authority. One who has never had the restrictions and confinement as well as the freedom and responsibility of being under authority is not prepared to rule. His interest will only be in his own gain, and he will sacrifice everything for it. When we submit to this authority, we develop the kind of character that qualifies us to be in authority. The life of Joseph in the Bible is an excellent example of this.

It is also important to note that every problem we find in this world has, at its heart, an authority issue. The tendency of man is to throw off the authority we are under, but to do so causes eternal damage and hinders our opportunities to be changed into the image of Christ. The disciplines learned under authority develop the character of a person who is at peace with himself and his environment. The conflict of our world is a reflection of the inner conflict we have with authority.

Staying on course is essential to walking by faith. Occasionally, however, it is necessary to look back to where we have come from to see where the Lord is leading us. This can be confusing unless we look only at the times in our lives when we responded to God with faith. Then it becomes clear. All manner of experiences occur in the life of a believer, but it is only the faith experiences that reveal the Lord and His work. "For therein is the righteousness of God revealed from faith to faith..."[28] The result of taking a step of faith is not to *achieve* the righteousness of God but to *reveal* the God of righteousness, and it is accomplished with each faith experience. Simply put, evangelism is impossible except there be an exposing of the righteousness of God in the Christian through his faith. Let me illustrate: When a person repents of his sinful condition and places his faith in Jesus as his Lord, he has a faith experience (represented by **F**). Immediately, Satan will try to add the believer's works to the formula of faith (represented by **W**). The average Christian's experience might look something like this: **F – W – W – W – F – W – W**–and it might sound something like this:

---

[28] Romans 1:17

Suppose there is a man who surrenders control of his life to Christ. (**F**) At this point, the Lord forgives him of his sin, and he feels much better. He wants to please God but fails to understand that, without faith, it is impossible because whatsoever is not of faith is sin. He understands that he is saved but believes that he must now show effort (**W**). He is sincere in his desire but wrong in his understanding that effort pleases God and, as a result, falls on his face in his attempt to do right. He wrongly believes that he hasn't tried hard enough, so he gives it his best effort (**W**) and again is met with defeat. Finally, he stops trusting his effort and trusts the Lord for direction (**F**) and the Lord forgives him. Now that he is forgiven and feels much better, he believes that, although he faltered the first time, he will be very careful to avoid the same trap (**W**) and again fails in his attempt to please God because he focuses on his works. He may go back and forth for many years before he understands the truth that our effort does not contribute to our righteousness. In fact, it displeases God. What pleases God is faith, and it pleases him because his righteousness is revealed through it.[29] Each time we exercise our faith in the Lord, we expose the righteousness of God. The rest of the time we obscure it. It is not uncommon to fail in trying to please the Lord, but it requires a deliberate and purposeful agreeing of one's heart to the revealed will of God.

The condition of man

There are untold numbers of people who are trying to find solutions to the problems in their lives but do not know what is wrong with them. As a wise man once said, *you can't fix something until you know what's broken.* And as the world attempts to find solutions, their efforts go in all directions. We try to buy ourselves out of trouble but discover we are bankrupt. We try to excuse our actions, but we cannot accept the same actions in others. We try various religions, but their gods do not respond. We work harder and longer. We spend more, and nothing seems to work. Could it be that we are trying to fix the wrong things?

Our major problem is not environmental or hereditary, economic, governmental, social or physical. It is a *sin* problem. Sin is a reality

---

[29] The phrase, *from faith unto faith*, in Romans 1:17 speaks to this.

whether or not we accept it. It is always destructive and ultimately ends in death. It's like the cartoon character, Pogo, who said, "We have met the enemy and he is us."

Before we can really face the sin problem, we must define sin. This is a point of confusion with the saved and lost alike. First, it's important to recognize that there is a big difference between *sin* and *sins*. Sin is a heart condition of self-sufficiency, and sins are what you do as a result of that condition. John the baptizer declared of Jesus, "Behold the Lamb of God, who taketh away the sin of the world." Notice that he did not say that He taketh away the *sins* of the world. It is one sin that causes all our problems, and it resides in the heart. Because of this, we do all manner of sins.

Consider the passages that follow one of the most often quoted verses in the Bible: John 3:17 and 18. Here, God explains that no one goes to heaven because of what he does but because of what he believes, and no one goes to hell because of what he does but because of what he refuses to believe. If it were on the standard of works, it would be unfair and impossible, but because it is on the standard of faith, it is both fair and possible. Faith is something that everyone can do equally.[30] God is not interested in punishment but redemption. Culpability is a fact that we cannot deny. However, it's not the fact that we are guilty that God is concerned with, but whether or not we will receive His remedy. It's like a man falling from an airplane without a parachute. The fall is not what kills him. In fact, some people do it for recreation. What kills him is the sudden stop. Still, the fall of man alone doesn't seal his fate, but if he refuses to accept or use the parachute offered by the blood of Jesus, his life ends in death. The blood of Jesus is God's only remedy for sin.[31] Nothing else will do. Death is unnecessary, but it will surely happen if we fail to accept God's remedy.

God's confrontation of man

After Adam had sinned in the Garden of Eden, he tried to hide his sin by hiding and making an apron of fig leaves. He didn't want

---

[30] The word faith and the word believe use exactly the same root word in the Greek language.

[31] Hebrews 9:22

to face the truth about himself. That is why the Lord called him in the cool of the day. "Adam, Adam, where art thou?" It's not that the Lord didn't know where he was. It was Adam who didn't know where he was. The Lord was bringing Adam to face himself and his sin. Richard Feynman, a Nobel Prize winning physicist once said, "you must not fool yourself – and you are the easiest person to fool." No matter how painful or ugly, you must face yourself. Until you know your own heart, you will not do anything about it.

You may be curious about your heart's condition and even suspect that there is some adjustment that is needed, but you still cannot properly appraise your condition until the Lord reveals it to you. It was the Lord who confronted Adam, and it is the Holy Spirit that convicts men of sin today.

And when He is come, He will reprove the world of sin, and of righteousness, and of judgment: Of sin, because they believe not on Me; Of righteousness, because I go to my Father, and ye see me no more; Of judgment, because the prince of this world is judged. I have yet many things to say unto you, but ye cannot bear them now. Howbeit when He, the Spirit of truth, is come, He will guide you into all truth: for He shall not speak of himself; but whatsoever He shall hear, that shall He speak: and He will shew you things to come. [32]

It is not until you understand that you are incapable of saving yourself that you will look to another. You must see sin for what it is and what it does. Anything less will lead you to a compromise and certain death. It may seem strange to consider, but imagine the possibility that, if you really wanted to, you could have slept with a rattlesnake last night. Most rational people wouldn't want to, and it is the same with rejecting sin. We will not have the desire to reject sin until we see it for what it is. However, when we see sin as a deadly and destructive force in our lives, we will most certainly reject it as quickly as we would reject sleeping with a rattlesnake. In religious circles, this is called repentance of sin. Repentance is not something that you come to on your own. It is not something that someone can

---

[32] John 16:8-13

convince you to do. The Holy Spirit alone is responsible for it. The best we can do is to pray and ask that the Holy Spirit awaken a man to his sin.

God's conformation of man

In the modern world, we often hear that actions have consequences, and it was no less true in the Garden of Eden. Consider Genesis 3:1, where God confronts Adam. "Because thou hast . . . cursed is the ground for thy sake." God knew what Adam had done. What is more, he knew what the results would be if He had done nothing. When we are confronted with our sin, it is overwhelming because God's judgment against sin is more than we can bear. However, without God's intervention, hope is lost. God had already promised a Savior who would bruise the head of Satan,[33] thus giving hope. He had further tied Eve's future to Adam, extending this hope even further.[34] Adam rejected God's will in favor of his own, and that brought consequences on himself and humanity. There is the ultimate consequence of death and the immediate consequence of the cursing of the ground. Man has already suffered the consequence of the death (spiritual separation) of their relationship and now faces a tough life because the ground is cursed.

It might seem strange to think that God would curse the ground "for thy sake," but our benefit is precisely what He has in mind because struggle aids in our development. There is a well-known story about an individual who was watching a butterfly come out of its cocoon. As the butterfly worked its way out, it came to a point where it seemed as though it just couldn't make it, so the man decided to help by cutting away the cocoon. The butterfly was soon out and walking around. The man then noticed that the butterfly was disproportional. Its body was larger than normal, and its wings were smaller. It was doomed to walk and never fly. In his effort to make it easier for the butterfly to escape, he cheated the butterfly of the very process that would allow the wings to develop so that it could fly. That restriction was for the butterfly's good, and so it is with us. It is the struggle that enables us to change. If we always take the easy

---

[33] Genesis 3:15
[34] Genesis 3:16

31

way, we will always be settling for the lesser blessings. It is often said that *rivers and men become crooked by taking the easy way.*

The Old Testament Law was never intended to save anyone.[35] Its purpose was to teach us our need of Christ so that we would be justified by our faith in Him alone and not because of our own merit. The law is our cocoon. It doesn't produce life. It just causes us to develop so that we can enjoy it.

The first way God has chosen to develop man is through struggle, and the second is through the law. There is a third means that God has chosen, and that is found in Romans 12:1-2:

> *I beseech you therefore, brethren, by the mercies of God, that ye present your bodies a living sacrifice, holy, acceptable unto God, which is your reasonable service. And be not conformed to this world: but be ye transformed by the renewing of your mind, that ye may prove what is that good, and acceptable, and perfect, will of God*

The word transformed is the Greek word *metamorphoo* (met-am-or-fo'-o), which literally means to change, or to transform. This is the same word that describes the process of change from a worm to a butterfly. God's intention is to change us from creatures of sin into sons, from temporal to eternal, worldly to spiritual, slaves of sin to servants, defeated to victorious, lost to saved, and flawed to perfect in Christ. God is in the conforming business.[36] For those who choose Christ of their own volition, God has set aside and guaranteed their completion into the image of Jesus. This guarantee is backed by the wisdom, power and treasuries of God Himself.

Lest you be discouraged by your own weakness, look at John 1:12. "But as many as received Him, to them gave He power to become the sons of God, even to them that believe on His name." Those who are on a faith standard of living and have been born from above have the guarantee that all of the power that is needed to be

---

[35] Wherefore the law was our schoolmaster to bring us unto Christ, that we might be justified by faith. Galatians 3:4

[36] For whom He did foreknow, He also did predestinate to be conformed to the image of His Son, that He might be the firstborn among many brethren. Romans 8:29

changed is available to them. This power for becoming is unlimited. God will spare no expense when it comes to His children being transformed. God will not accept inferior product in His work either. That is why He rejected all works of the flesh. Salvation is of God and not man. We are His workmanship, and as such, we can expect nothing less than complete victory.[37]

God's confirmation of man

After Adam had sinned, was confronted and judged, God did something very unexpected. He killed an animal and used its skin to make clothes for Adam and Eve. One must wonder why God would feel the need to do such a thing. From Scripture we know that Adam and Eve were naked prior to the sin, and it was not a problem at that time. After their sin, we find that they attempted to make a covering for themselves.

No covering was needed prior to the sin because there was no issue between God and man. Once man sinned, he usurped God's authority and attempted to take control for himself. His fig leaf clothing represented his attempt to take charge. By making a covering for his nakedness, he was attempting to solve the problem himself, without God. Before their sin, there was nothing hidden and nothing to hide. Now man was attempting to skirt the judgment of sin to avoid the death that Satan said he would surely not face.

When God confronted man with his sin, he found that his fig leaf covering did nothing to hide him. Stripped of his best efforts, man stood before God fully exposed. God then judges the sin of the serpent, the woman and the man.

An animal was sacrificed in order to provide man with a covering for his nakedness. Here is the picture of how God intends to deal with man's sin. He will spill the blood of the innocent to preserve the guilty. The skin of the lamb that was given to man was a picture of God's protective covering. This picture was so impressed upon Adam that quite probably he continued to observe the rite of blood sacrifice, and that is how Able knew to sacrifice the firstling of his flock. That man continued to observe the rite of blood sacrifice was his expression of faith and confirmation that he would rely on

---

[37] Ephesians 2:10

God's provision for sin and not his own. His wearing of animal skins that God had provided was the symbol of his surrender again to the authority of God. Such is the picture of a man restored to fellowship with God, under authority and walking by faith in the Lord and His Word.

The Scripture in Genesis 3:22-24 is often misunderstood. Generally, it is read as "now that man has created such a mess, I'll make sure he never has access to the Tree of Life again." This couldn't be further from the truth. God didn't give up on man but rather preserved the way back to the Tree of Life. Notice that God's action was based upon man becoming like God in the sense that he then knew the difference between good and evil. The problem was that if man would have taken from the Tree of Life in that condition of sin, he would have been permanently separated from God. God never intended for man to live without Him. Man was created for the purpose of fellowshipping with God forever. To accomplish this, he placed the angel with the flaming sword at the entrance to the Tree of Life to protect man from prematurely taking from it and being permanently formed without Him. The way is kept open and available to whosoever will come by faith and take freely. Faith is the pavement on the road back to God.[38]

---

[38] It is not God's will that any perish, but that all come to repentance. II Peter 3:9

Chapter 4

The Operation of Faith

Looking unto Jesus the author and finisher of our faith
– Hebrews 12:2

Jesus said unto him, If thou canst believe, all things are possible to him that believeth
– Mark 9:23

As I began to prepare for the ministry, I asked my pastor to recommend a school. He said that he didn't know of any schools worth recommending at that time, as there was so much liberal teaching going on. I was shocked by his answer, but I was certain that there was a place for me and continued to pray that the Lord would make a way.

About this time, the Lord moved a man who lived in Florida to sell his business and move to Colorado. This same man joined our church and told me about a school in Kentucky that was just for preachers. They employed their students by making church furniture, provided housing that was affordable even to students, and assisted in finding opportunities to minister and preach. It was clear that they took care of their students and made provisions for their families. It seemed that God's fingerprints were all over it, so I sent off for the school catalogue. I promptly returned my application and other required documents, but when I didn't hear from them at the start of the semester, I began to wonder if my application had gotten lost in the mail. I continued my preparations to go and still worked in the church and at my regular day job. In October, I sold all of our furniture to a neighbor and said good-bye to our friends and family.

On the way, we stopped at my uncle's home to visit. The second day we were there I got a phone call from the school. They first explained that I should not forward my mail to the school, and when I asked why, they said that it was because I hadn't been accepted yet. They also said that I wouldn't be able to come to the school on the expectation of being accepted at a later time because there was no housing available, no work, and no one to help. Each time they tried to dissuade me from coming, I simply said that these were God's problems, and I was simply obeying what he had revealed for me to do. But with each reply they continued in their efforts to convince me that it was a mistake to continue my journey. Finally, I asked if they would simply hold my mail until I arrived, and they agreed.

It was Thanksgiving Day when we finally drove into town. We immediately got a room at a motel. On Sunday morning we had no idea where to go to church. We spread out the newspaper and prayed that the Lord would direct us to the right church. After reviewing a number of churches, we came to one that looked right. We had a sense of confirmation about it, so that is where we went. When we got to the church, however, my wife was feeling sick due to her pregnancy, and she stayed in the car. I went inside and found a pew almost halfway up the aisle and sat near the middle. Not knowing anyone, I just sat there quietly and prayed and read from my Bible. The service went well, and I felt a spiritual connection. As soon as the service was over, I quickly made my way out to check on my wife. The pastor caught me at the exit and asked my name but got little more, as I hurried out. We went back to our room and checked our funds. We had enough money to pay the motel and a few meals for two more days.

We drove out to the school the following day in hopes that we could speak to one of the administrators. As soon as the word got out that we were there, the president of the school sent a message that he would like to see me. I went to his office, and he began by telling me that I had created quite a stir on campus. He reminded me that I had not yet been accepted, that no housing was available, there were no jobs in the area, and that I didn't have anyone to help. I replied that he was correct. He then asked if our finances were low, and I again said that was correct. Then he asked me what my plans were, and I simply said that I was following the Lord as well as I could understand Him. Whether or not I was to go to school was the Lord's decision. If not, it was fine with me, but if so, He would take care of the details.

By Friday of that week, the Lord had provided everything that we needed. What I didn't know at the time was that the school had a policy that students would not be allowed to enroll mid-year, only at the beginning of the fall term. I was the first exception. In a place where no housing was available, one of the students moved out of student housing that week to take a church with a parsonage. Before we could even look at the cottage, the student body who had heard of us by then had fully furnished our new home. In the meantime, we were given meals at the school kitchen and temporary accommodations for two nights in a guest room. The school had even given me a job on the work program for 20 hours a week.

On Sunday we returned to the same church we attended the week before. At the end of the service, the pastor called my wife and me by name and asked us to come to the front of the church. We were very surprised and a little uneasy that he had called on us at the end of the service, but we complied. The pastor explained that after our visit the previous week, the Lord had laid a burden on the church to help our family and that they had something in the kitchen for us. As they led us back to the kitchen, I thought that they probably had a few groceries for us and that this was a nice gesture. As we entered the kitchen, I couldn't believe what I was seeing. There were boxes of food covering two tables; full boxes on the counter and under the table. I leaned on one of the doorjambs and broke down crying uncontrollably for several minutes. The people were so patient. They quietly waited for me to finish. Finally, I got control of myself, and the pastor continued by saying, "And some of the people didn't hear about it in time and they wanted in on it." Then he grabbed my hand and placed a large roll of money in it. I broke down again. It was some time before I was able to get control of myself again, and then one of the members said, "I didn't get in on it, either" and several others joined him in handing us more money. They even handed money to our children. God's supply, through this church, was one of the greatest outpourings of love to us that I have ever experienced.

I cannot tell you what this experience did for me. Every barrier to us was broken down. Every need supplied. God was at work. My faith in Him grew beyond what I could imagine. It has led me through times when I could not see. I learned that circumstances do not determine the will of God, that you need God-sized problems to see God-sized power. It is not until the problems become greater than we can handle that most of us will release them to God.

I also learned that when you are trusting God, you are not looking for a particular result. I didn't know how the Lord was going to work or what He was going to do. All I knew was that I trusted Him and that whatever happened was okay with me. I never assumed that I would go to this school. I never thought that it wasn't going to be hard. I only thought about walking straight. The outcome was up to God, and I was willing to face anything with Him. Submission to the Lord is essential to walking by faith.

All of us long to have this kind of experience and perhaps much of the frustration of our attempts to walk by faith come because we do not discern that there is a specific order of operation governing faith in God that is revealed in Scripture. To change or omit any of the parts of the operation of faith would mean that it would not produce the intended results. This operation is essential to induce God's involvement. So that we might not make the same mistake, let's look at the operation of faith and its order. First God initiates, then man believes and finally God performs.

God initiates

This is where our faith begins. It does not originate with man. Faith is a means whereby we participate in what God is doing, not what we direct God to do. After God has revealed His will for us, we are to then choose it for ourselves. This is where the fight of faith takes place. Once we come to the settled position that we stand on faith in Christ alone, God works His wonder, and we behold His glory.

Scriptural faith does not begin or end with man, but with God.[39] The problem begins when we attempt to initiate faith. Man has a depraved nature, and it is ever vying for control.[40] It wants to be in charge to gratify itself. Self-centeredness is at the very heart of sin and will ultimately destroy everything it possesses. It operates on a flawed premise, that self-gratification will bring ultimate fulfillment. However, this will never produce the desired result. God alone can initiate biblical faith. He is the author. If we miss it at this point, it is not scriptural faith, for it must be faith in God. You cannot and will not trust Him until you are responding to His initiative.

There is a quick, three point test that you can apply to verify that your faith is faith in God. 1. Does it contradict the Scriptures at any point? The Scriptures neither contradict themselves nor God but are in complete harmony. We must stand on what the Scriptures say for they have stood the test of time and attack. 2. Does it agree with the witness of the Spirit of God in you? If you know better inside, you would be standing against yourself to proceed. Jesus said that a kingdom divided against itself cannot stand.[41] 3. Does it align with what other saints have proved over the ages? The success of those who proved the will of God will light the way for us who follow. "Examine yourselves, whether ye be in the faith; prove your own selves. Know ye not your own selves, how that Jesus Christ is in you, except ye be reprobates?" [42]

All manner of error develops from the mistake of initiating the action. For example, we do not have the privilege to "name it and claim it." That teaching begins with man and his desires. It makes everything subject to our own whim. Even Jesus said "I can of mine own self, do nothing."[43] If Jesus would not let His human desires direct His affairs, then how much more important is it that we wait upon the Lord? Faith is not a tool to manipulate God but an avenue to join Him.

---

[39] Looking unto Jesus the author and finisher of our faith. Hebrews 12:2

[40] Jeremiah 17:9

[41] Mark 3:24, Luke 11:17

[42] II Corinthians 13:5

[43] John 5:30

Problems in faith do not occur because of some flaw in our new nature but because our old nature is not subdued. Though we have been crucified with Christ, it takes a lifetime for our old nature to fully die. Although we are in the habit of being in control, we dare not trust ourselves, for we are not qualified or equipped to find our own way. Further, when we are the initiator, the glory is ours, and we are in control. When God is the initiator, He becomes the focus of the experience, and He is in control. Faith must begin with God; otherwise, we rely totally upon ourselves. It would be as though we could somehow pick ourselves up by our bootstraps and lift ourselves into the heavens. Faith, by definition, is reliance upon someone or something other than ourselves.

If you don't need God's involvement, why make the pretense of faith? On the other hand, if you do need His involvement, why would you trust only yourself? Isn't it self evident that you need the Lord to direct your way?

Not only did He open the way of faith to the Christian, but He also closed all other options. Romans 14:23 says, "For whatsoever is not of faith is sin." The Lord does not intend for us to operate outside of faith. He will work within faith, but outside of faith, nothing but correction is promised to the Christian.

It is important to note that the reason God requires us to walk by faith is to bless us.[44],[45],[46] God has only good planned for us. It is our depraved mind and nature that tells us He is like us, and we should watch out for Him. If we really knew how He longs to share His blessings with us, we would not be suspicious of Him.

Man believes

The second arena of faith is man believing. Our everyday understanding of *believe* is centered on the idea of conviction or accepting something as true; however, The distinction between how man defines belief and what the Scriptures teach is often contradictory. The Scripture knows nothing of a faith in God that originates or is directed by man. To get God's perspective you must go to God's

---

[44] It is not God's will that any perish but that all come to repentance. Matthew 18:14

[45] It is the Father's good pleasure to give you the kingdom. Luke 12:32

[46] I am come that ye might have life and have it more abundantly. John 10:10b

word. A good place to begin is the gospel of John. You will find that the word appears numerous times and includes the idea of commitment to Jesus as Lord. You cannot trust Him with eternity without also trusting Him with the present. If you will not trust Him in your present circumstance, how can you trust Him with eternity, which is being established even at this very moment?

The operation of faith creates a problem for us in that we aren't comfortable with being dependent on God, as our nature is to be independent; however, the sooner we correct this point, the sooner we can continue with our faith walk. "There is a way which seemeth right unto a man, but the end thereof are the ways of death."[47] We have it in our heads that we know best and that somehow God is out of touch. Man thinks that he knows the right way, just as he thought he did in the Garden of Eden. In his attempt to take charge, he invariably chooses the path of destruction. This is why salvation is by grace through faith.[48] Just as a person is saved through faith, he lives by faith.[49] The principle of faith is the means to salvation, and the same principle by which we live our lives as Christians. We are to move from faith experience to faith experience and thereby expose the righteousness of God.[50]

When we came to trust Jesus as Lord, we did so because we came to the point that we lost confidence in our own judgment. We recognized how sin had taken hold of our lives and was destroying the very essence of life itself. In desperation, we turned to the Lord, and He saved us. Invariably we think, *now that I am saved, I will resume control but this time I will do better.* This ends in utter failure, and we desperately turn again to the Lord, who again rescues us. This process will repeat itself again and again until the believer learns that the way is by faith and not by sight. We try to get God to work another way, but He will not move on this issue. We can beg, bargain, pout, plead, threaten, reason, assert, petition, request and argue, but God only responds to faith. Although He does not respond

---

[47] Proverbs 14:12

[48] Ephesians 2:10

[49] Galatians 2:20

[50] Romans 1:17

to any other means, He will always respond to faith in Jesus. This is His chosen means of operation. To use any other means is sin. [51], [52]

Some people have the mistaken idea that we are working for God. The truth is that God is working for us. God doesn't need help, but we do. God doesn't need us to do anything. He is quite capable on his own. What He does want for us is to be developed into all that He has planned for us. This development comes about every time we venture out by faith. We trust the Lord and discover how wrong we were in our understanding and how right God is. Point by point we dismantle our old way of thinking and living and more and more our testimony becomes as it is written in Acts 17:28a: "It is in Him that we live and move and have our being".

The application of faith to circumstances is also a struggle to the natural mind. Quite often believers understand that God is operating in their lives, but they wonder if they should simply sit back and wait for things to come about, or if they should take initiative to make certain events happen. Both of these options are wrong. The first would excuse man's responsibility, and the second would assume all of the responsibility. The correct answer is to remain in the position of faith, and you may do whatever is consistent within that position.

Let me illustrate the operation of faith as a person making his first trip on an airplane. Before believing is possible, there must first be a way (the plane itself illustrates the capacity for God to act). Then there is the struggle of believing. No plane can transport you to another destination until you get on board. Then it remains the task of the plane to do what it was designed to do: get you to your destination. As you know, the airline industry has made tremendous progress in the development of a system of travel that is beyond our ancestors' imaginations. However, knowing that a system is capable of doing a task does not complete the task. One must be willing to trust it to the point of full commitment by getting on board. Unless this is done, nothing is accomplished. However, once on board, one is further required to stay on board. This is greatly misunderstood when it comes to faith. Some will tell you that you must not doubt or it will spoil faith, as in James 1;6-7:

---

[51] For whatsoever is not of faith is sin Romans 14:23b

[52] For without faith it is impossible to please Him. Hebrews 11:6

But let him ask in faith, nothing wavering. For he that wavereth is like a wave of the sea driven with the wind and tossed. For let not that man think that he shall receive any thing of the Lord.

The wavering in these verses correlates to getting on and off the plane and deals with commitment, not mental questions. Others will tell you that you must understand what you are doing or it isn't going to work. However, that would mean that it is my faith that does the work instead of God. Still others will tell you that you must not fear or it isn't faith, but consider our analogy. Once on board, all that is required is that I remain in my seat until I arrive at my destination. Fear, doubt, or lack of understanding as to the laws of physics have no effect on an airplane's ability to fly. The same thing is true with faith. It will work even if we are scared, confused and bewildered, so long as we maintain our position of trust in the Lord to do the work and do not take it into our own hands.

It is not your job to figure out how God is going to work in your life. Your job is to believe what the Lord has said.[53] The possibilities are only limited by the will of God. If you can believe it, you can see it come to pass. It is not a magic trick, an illusion or some crafty way to manipulate God. It is not an empty promise that only a few special people can achieve. This is God's promised way of working to provide us with the things we need to grow up in Him. God has already willed to provide it when He asked us to believe it. It does not require works of the flesh to accomplish it. In fact, these hinder the work of God. It only requires the kinds of faith works that are necessary to hold us in a position of trust and obedience.

The Bible makes much of the importance of the task of believing. There are literally hundreds of references to faith and believing. We tend to diminish its importance, but it is so important to God that he spared nothing to open the way of life to us, which is by faith. Everything else is secondary to this one task. It is so important to God that He has elected to limit His working with man to the operation of faith. He is ever speaking, but His will is not accomplished because we are not mature in faith. God is not looking for great men.

---

[53] A word of caution: make sure He is the one who said it and no other.

43

He is looking for men of great faith, men who dare to believe what He has said. These are the men God will use to do mighty things.

God performs

We now come to the final arena of God following through on His promise. We began this study in the arena of God working for man and then moved to the arena where man was trusting God. Now we are back to God's arena where He finishes what He started. The Lord's intention is not to find out if you will obey, as He already knows the answer from the beginning. His plan in bringing you to this impossible situation is to change your understanding in multiple ways, to paint a picture through your experience of faith of the nature and essence of God to the world, and to manifest His glory of power and love to man.

A change in our understanding:

Perhaps the most obvious result is what happens to us. Our venture of faith began with a revelation from God. It was all new to us and very foreign. It violated our reason and extended beyond our means. The only reason that we ventured out is that it was God who extended the invitation.[54] So we accepted the invitation and stood firm in the position of faith, seeing God move heaven and earth if necessary to bring it to pass. Now we are reflecting upon the past events and have come to some amazing conclusions: We were wrong about what natural man's instincts insisted was true. Our original evaluation was flawed because of what we didn't know and could not see. God really was looking out for us and seeking to bless us. God's way really is best, and we have more confidence in Him than we ever had before. With what we have learned, we have more confidence in our relationship to the Lord, and we can respond to life better. We love the Lord more than we ever have before. We look forward to our next venture of faith. These are just some of the normal responses.

---

[54] Like Peter walking on water.

A Picture:

The next thing that happens is the picture of God is exposed. Romans 1:16-17 tells us that God can be seen in the believer whenever he operates by faith in God.[55] The world is cut off from a clear view of God because of their sin. We act as a mirror for them to see God, a view otherwise impossible for them. When they behold the glory of God, their sin becomes exceedingly sinful. Until then, they only have other sinful men to compare themselves with and feel that they are doing as good as anyone else.

His Glory:

The third thing that happens is that God is glorified. That simply means that God is exposed to us, and our appraisal of Him has increased in value. It does not mean that His value has gone up but that our value of Him has gone up. He is greater than we had ever imagined. God is already infinite in glory. He is not on some ego trip that He needs praise to bolster Himself. He wants us to know Him as He is. If we were to do the work of healing or miracles, others would look to us. But we are not the answer. He is. Our job is to point others to Him. Also, people will turn to God when they see Him working successfully with man. Who would want to fly in an airline with a poor safety record? And who would trust God when so many Christians blow up in mid-flight? Let your light so shine before men, that they may see your good works (of faith), and glorify your Father, which is in heaven.[56]

One final note: Just because faith does not follow the way that seemeth right, this does not mean that we are to follow anything that seems wrong. There are deceivers a plenty that would say that you should throw reason out the window since reason isn't a reliable path. I am not advocating such practices. The Lord has given us His word, and nothing should be allowed that contradicts it. He has given us His Spirit who is charged to lead us, teach us and guide us into all truth. He has also given us our victories of faith. They are

---

[55] For I am not ashamed of the gospel of Christ, for it is the power of God unto salvation to everyone that believeth; to the Jew first, and also to the Greek. For therein is the righteousness of God revealed from faith unto faith: as it is written, the just shall live by faith.

[56] Matthew 5:16

precious to us and cannot be denied. He has also given us gifted men who we are to counsel, those who are recognized as walking in the faith. There is safety in the counsel of the godly.

The Bible references *the gifted*, which are those men who are given to the church for the perfecting of the saints.[57], [58] The church leadership is charged with this counsel and must answer to the Lord for their guidance. In addition to leaders of the church, there are those who are recognized and spiritual leaders who have demonstrated wise counsel in the past and who the Lord has brought into your life. They may be denominational leaders, missionaries, ministers to specific needs, chaplains, Christian teachers or family members. It is important to remember that they are to be gifted men that are spirit-directed, and not just holding a position. We can also find counsel in the great men of faith in the past, such as the church fathers, Martin Luther, Tyndale, George Muller and Charles Finney. Another source of counsel is found in the work of the men of God in today's age, such as Billy Graham, Charles Stanley, Chuck Swindoll and Adrian Rogers, to name a few.

We learned in Chapter One that faith is not quantifiable. Sometimes we hear phrases like, *enough faith*, which is erroneous as it is in reference to the degree or amount of faith, as though some faith works and some does not. It isn't faith that works. It is the Lord. Although the Bible speaks of little faith and great faith, these phrases speak of the maturity level of faith the believer has in the Lord and not in the amount of faith the believer possesses. Faith is a way of expressing our confidence in the Lord, and our confidence grows as we discover the trustworthiness of God. Faith is built on the knowledge of the Lord. The more you know Him, the more you will trust Him. The way to grow in maturity is to go through a God-sized problem, one that requires a God-sized answer. When you have trusted Him, you will have faith to continue on. Each faith venture builds faith in God and enables us to trust Him more than we did before. Faith has always been God's method of operation and will be the basis of operation in eternity. We had better get used to it.

---

[57] Ephesians 4
[58] Hebrews 13:17

46

Chapter 5

The Steps of Faith

Who also walk in the steps of that faith of our father Abraham, which he had being yet uncircumcised.

– Romans 4:12

That ye should follow in His steps.

– I Peter 2:21c

The *steps of faith* are those choices that we make to reject the way that seems right to man[59] and instead trust in the Lord's revelation. When Adam sinned, the special relationship with God ceased to exist, and he was left to continue in the best way he knew how. He had become the director of his own life, and that tendency to function independently is inherent in all of us. This self-life is at the heart of all sin and is the cause of all of our sinful actions.

Sin is not what you do, for that is the product of sin; rather, sin is what you are and the motive of all of your actions. Not only is this the barrier to our having a right relationship with God, it is the reason Jesus came to remove the barrier of sin so our relationship could be restored. Those choices are what the Lord uses in conforming us to the image of Christ. When we surrender the control of our lives back to God (in the person of Jesus), we move to a new level of operation as we confront life's situations.

---

[59] Proverbs 14:12

Sometimes those steps will be relatively easy, as our will is easy to mold. Sometimes those steps will be difficult because we resist trusting the Lord. One thing to remember is that the more difficult it is to trust the Lord, the more you will gain by trusting Him.

We must be careful not to equate an experience with a step of faith. We may repeat an experience many times and in many different ways without changing our faith. It's not a step of faith until we alter our response from operating by sight –by worldly understanding– to a position of trusting Him on a new level and then proceeding with the new methodology.

Every believer will go through different experiences, yet the steps require the same response: release one's grip on the world system and surrender to the control of Christ. The order will generally follow the same path; however, the order may be altered for specific lessons that the Lord may choose for an individual. It is also important to note that not everyone will learn the same things about each step. What you learn will depend on what the Lord has specifically designed for you.[60] Some people try to skip some of the steps but later find that they have to go back before they can go forward. If they are unwilling to do the first work, they cannot do the second. You simply cannot cheat in faith. You have to grow in grace and knowledge. Your growth rate is dependent upon the plan the Lord has for your life and your response of faith to Him. Stubbornness, refusal, self-will, and pride will slow down your pace while surrender, obedience, and faithfulness will move you forward. The only way to get to be 21 years of age is to live 21 years, and the only way to become mature in faith is to take the steps of faith, one at a time. You can accelerate the pace, but you cannot change the route.

The specific steps that you will go through are dependent on what areas of your life are yielded to the Lord and what areas you hold as your area of control. The areas that you maintain control of are especially important, as they are something that you will need to resolve in order for you to grow in your faith. God never sends us where he has not prepared us in faith. He will not call us to a work that our faith in Him will not support. You cannot achieve spiritually beyond your faith in the Lord.

---

[60] Psalms 37:23

Before any understanding of faith is possible, one must establish a spiritual mind and heart that is capable of receiving God's teaching. No amount of scholarship is adequate to comprehend spiritual things. This relationship begins with an act of God upon an individual in which he receives the perfect translator, the Holy Spirit, into his heart and life. This act is known by several names. We call it the *New Birth*, or *Born Again*, *Regeneration*, being *justified* or *getting saved*. Whatever name you use, it speaks of one act of God upon the believer who has faced his own sinful heart and repented or turned away from its supremacy and surrendered to the Lordship of Jesus. Until this event has taken place, there is no avenue to receive spiritual understanding.[61] We may have great knowledge about this world and yet be ignorant as to what God is doing or what He has willed.

The Holy Spirit is our teacher. We know nothing about spiritual things until the Holy Spirit teaches us. Everything learned spiritually is learned by revelation. It may come through scripture or prayer or through experience, but it is always because the Holy Spirit has revealed it.[62] This is why you are suddenly able to understand a passage from a whole new perspective, even though you have read it multiple times. There are some who do not understand this truth and try to gain knowledge of God's will through a different translation.[63] However, the Holy Spirit is not restricted by language, ability, culture, geography or other similar factors that normally

---

[61] But the natural man receiveth not the things of the Spirit of God; for they are foolishness to him; neither can he know them because they are spiritually discerned. I Corinthians 2:14

[62] Nevertheless I tell you the truth; It is expedient for you that I go away: for if I go not away, the Comforter will not come unto you; but if I depart, I will send him unto you. John 16:7
But the Comforter, which is the Holy Ghost, whom the Father will send in my name, he shall teach you all things, and bring all things to your remembrance, whatsoever I have said unto you. John 14:26
Howbeit when he, the Spirit of truth, is come, he will guide you into all truth: for he shall not speak of himself; but whatsoever he shall hear, that shall he speak: and he will shew you things to come. John 16:13

[63] This does not mean that different versions of the Bible are inherently flawed by virtue of the fact that they are translations. The problem is referencing different translations as a path to revelation, instead of the Holy Spirit.

frame our understanding of the natural world. The Holy Spirit is restricted only by our stubborn refusal to confront and confess our sin. Consider that even the most basic of all truths, such as John 3:16, is realized only when the Holy Spirit reveals it. That is why not everyone who reads scripture has revelation. If the heart is unmoved from its position of sin, revelation cannot be received.

It is essential that we not only establish the capacity to receive truth but also maintain that relationship by a renewal of the mind.[64] A person may become a Christian and have the Holy Spirit reveal truth to him but become worldly and have that avenue clogged with sin. When this happens, even the truth that he has thus far discerned becomes confused with the emotion of the worldly man, and its meaning is lost. The problem with this condition is that he may not be aware of it until some time later. He may think that there is no problem or issue because he doesn't sense the change. However, anyone who is not actively being renewed in the Spirit of his mind is becoming carnal or worldly. In order to continually receive revelation from the Holy Spirit, you must be continually renewing the Spirit of your mind.

When a Christian begins to move into a worldly state, the Holy Spirit will endeavor to correct his course. It may range from a gentle reminder to a severe reprimand, depending on the condition of the heart and its willingness to turn.[65], [66] All of us need this correction, and it is a continual process. It is important to note the Lord is not interested in punishing the Christian for his failings, only to correct and restore them. Every discipline is redemptive in its purpose and aids in our being turned toward the Lord.

The New birth

The first step of faith for every believer is the new birth. This has been addressed elsewhere in this book, and I do not want to be repetitive in describing how it happens. I simply want to point out

---

[64] Romans 12:1-2

[65] As many as I love, I rebuke and chasten: be zealous therefore, and repent. Revelation 3:19

[66] But if ye be without chastisement, whereof all are partakers, then are ye bastards, and not sons. Hebrews 12:8

the role of faith in this experience. Prior to becoming a believer in the Lord, a person is a believer in something or someone else. This is his walk or way of life. He has developed a manner of living by which he orders his life. It is usually a combination of random pieces of thought, experience, philosophy, superstition, guess, desire, teaching, culture and the like, all mixed together that constitute an individual's personal way. Notice that there are several common denominators. First, there is the appeal to worldly reason. It relies on human conception, consideration and conclusion, without any regard to God. It is natural and has to fit natural law. Second is the appeal to the emotions. It relies on how a person feels and whether they feel right about their decision. There is also the appeal of self-preservation. (After all is said and done, how does it affect me?) Finally, there is the appeal to works. (My effort will earn me my way.[67]) However, the way that seems so right is destructive in the end. It's like a baited hook. It makes a desirable offer but comes with a hidden element that kills. As long as we look at the bait, we don't see the hook. We don't turn away until we see the full offer, which is death.

One of the two conditions for salvation is faith in the Lord Jesus (or to put it another way, faith in Jesus as Lord). The other condition is repentance of sin. The condition of faith will never be acknowledged as long as we retain confidence in the old way (self -government) as the final authority. We must come to the realization that *our way* leads to death and instead place our confidence in something that, although seems foreign and unnatural, is our only hope. It comes with multiple testimonies of others who have already made this choice and beacon us on. It comes with a promise from God and at a tremendous cost. Now, shaken from our weakness and past failures, and with hope in the Lord, we take the first step of faith and trust Jesus as our personal Lord and Savior.

Obedience
One of the surest signs that a person has truly been saved is the surrender of his will to obey the Scriptures and spiritual authorities

---

[67] For by grace are ye saved through faith; and that not of yourselves: it is the gift of God: Not of works, lest any man should boast. Ephesians 2:8-9

that are over him. If a person has faith in the Lord, he must reject everything that is against the Lord and His will and must accept whatever the Lord has revealed as His will. Obedience is not easy because there are at least three forces that insist on having their way: 1. the entire demonic host 2. the world system and 3. self-will or the demand to have our own way. This trio cannot be defeated without Divine intervention. We are powerless to overcome it, except when we walk in the Spirit. Untold numbers of people have wrecked their lives trying to overcome the flesh through self-will. The Scriptures say that if you walk in the Spirit, you will not fulfill the desires of the flesh.[68] Effort will not produce victory over self-will. It is not necessary that, when asked to obey, you understand the reason. You only need to know that it is the will of God, and then take the position of faith in Him, acknowledging He is in control of the events of your life.

Following the Lord in Baptism is one of the first things He commands us to obey. It is amazing how many people I run into that say they have become a Christian but have not been baptized, even after several years of professed salvation. Jesus asked, "Why do you call me Lord, Lord and do not the things I command?" If we will not follow the easiest and simplest commands, we are likely not to follow when the circumstances are more challenging. If we do not obey, we do not trust. It's as simple as that. The Lord will not accept our rationalizations and excuses. You either walk by faith or by sight, but you cannot please God except by faith in Him.

The Lord Jesus Himself had knowledge of who He was and His mission in this world at the age of 12. Luke 2:41ff says that Jesus was left in Jerusalem for three days. When Mary and Joseph found Him, he was in the temple, confounding the religious leaders. Now comes the question: why then did he spend another 18 years at home before starting His ministry? There are several pieces that go together to make up the answer. First, there is some indication that Joseph may have died during this time and Jesus, as the oldest son, took up the role of provider in his stead. Then there is the point of law that a man could not become a priest until he was 30 years of age. Jesus' ministry required Him to fulfill the office of a priest. Though He was

---

[68] Galatians 5:15.

not recognized as a priest by the Scribes and Pharisees of His day, Scripture acknowledges Him as our High Priest. Jesus demonstrated that obedience to the authority you are under is God's preparation for you to do His will. If it was necessary for Him to obey by faith, it is essential for us. A third reason is that, even though he was the Son of God, He still had to learn obedience for Himself [69] If it was true for Him who did not know sin, how much more necessary is it for us? Notice that obedience does not come naturally, but it must be learned. Notice also that it was learned through the things that He suffered. It is not enough for us to be secured for heaven. We must also learn obedience. This is even more important in an age where rejecting authority and rebellion are so commonplace.[70]

Stewardship

The third step of faith that we will examine is the step of stewardship. This step encompasses all areas of stewardship, including treasure, time, and talent. It is often said that spiritual truth is more caught than taught, meaning that we come to Spiritual truth through experience as much as study. As such, we might also refer to this step as the *illustrated version of faith*.

Treasures are material possessions, and money is the item of exchange for them. The Lord teaches us eternal truth through the material world. Treasures extend beyond money, but the principle of faith is the same for all treasures; therefore, I will illustrate the principle of faith with money and let you apply it to the rest of your treasures. Much has been written about money, and I do not intend to give a full treatment on the subject. What I intend to do is point out the role of faith in stewardship.

Money plays a big role in our lives because it touches so many areas. It defines our values and directs our activities. It represents the physical world. We spend most of our working time acquiring money. Money is not evil by itself. It is the love of money that is the root of all kinds of evil. Money is simply a tool of exchange and is necessary in most societies. It is both spiritual and scriptural to consider money when we look at our faith walk. The Bible speaks

---

[69] Hebrews 5:8

[70] See appendix 5.1

about money over 300 times, more than Heaven and Hell combined. If it is true that earning money comprises the majority of our waking time, it is easy to see why the Bible is so specific about its use. You could say that, if a man was not right with God in his finances, the majority of his life is not aligned with God.

Everything God created was a giver in the beginning. The ground, plants, animals and sun all give. In fact, man too was a giver in the beginning, before sin entered the picture. Ever since the first sin, man has been a taker, but in heaven it won't be that way. In heaven all will be givers again.

There is also the need to become a giver because that is the nature of God. He is the ultimate giver. He gave the best gift ever given, His Son. God's nature is giving, and if you are going to be like Him, then you will need to become a giver. You cannot enjoy full fellowship if your nature is contrary to His. We are to become like Him, and that includes becoming a giver. Consider the times you gave the most, when you did the best job, took the most care, went out of your way, or lifted someone up by a good word or helping hand. Weren't those the times when you felt the best inside? No one can take that away from you. That is what defines a man's heart. That is real reward. You can't buy it, borrow it or beg it. You can't get it, but you can give it, and it will last eternally. Jesus said, "In as oft as ye have done it to the least of these my brethren, ye have done it unto me."

In addition, there is the need to become a giver so that others might conceive something of God. It is worth repeating: giving is an act of faith. Romans 1:17 says that the righteousness of God is revealed from faith unto faith. Every time we exercise our faith in giving, others can catch a glimpse of God. The carnal world is grabbing, getting, taking and consuming. When they see you giving of yourself, it reveals a new way of living, something to which they are unaccustomed, and they want it.

And finally, there is the need to become a giver to access the blessings of God's provision. This is sometimes called *seed faith*. Let me illustrate this with a simplistic scenario. The national average of an American family is to spend 110% of their income. Let's say, for illustration, that your income is $100 and your expenses are $110. One might reason that if you used all of your income, you would be

$10 short. Furthermore, if you tithe, you would be $20 short. One might naturally conclude that they can't afford to tithe.

Now let's look at it with the *seed faith* principal. You give $10 to the Lord as an expression of your faith in Him, for He is your provision and not the $100. You are on the faith system, and it is up to Him to provide for you. Your faith in Him is the critical issue, not the paying of bills; therefore, you give $10. Your giving is the seed that you plant. You are faced with the dilemma that a farmer faces in the early spring. Does he eat the seed and hope it is enough to survive, or does he trust in a harvest and plant the seed? II Corinthians 9:16 says, "He that soweth sparingly shall reap sparingly, and he that soweth bountifully shall reap bountifully." The Bible teaches there is a harvest, and that harvest is in proportion to your faith. The Lord takes your seed and causes it to grow, even though you do not understand how. God's plan is thirtyfold for some, sixtyfold for others, or a hundred,[71] meaning that he multiplies the blessing by these amounts. Now you add that harvest to the 90%, and you have more than enough for your needs. "And God is able to make all grace abound toward you; that ye, always having all sufficiency in all things, may abound to every good work."[72] Instead of not being able to afford to give, it is the other way around: you can't afford *not* to give.

Consequently, the infamous question follows, "What about tithing?" First, it's important to understand that God doesn't want your money, and He doesn't need your money. It's not for His benefit but yours. You need to give because giving is an act of faith. I only use the above to illustrate the principle of seed faith. I don't believe that 10% is God's; I believe that 100% is God's. It all belongs to Him. We are stewards of His possessions. Whatever He asks us to do is a promise that we can do it.

Consider Mr. Turner, who invented Turner Dozer and became a multimillionaire, and Mr. Penny who started the J C Penny chain stores and also became a multimillionaire. God asked them to give 90% and live on 10%. I am not saying that if you give 90% then you will become a rich man. I am saying that you can live on any

---

[71] Mark 4:8

[72] II Corinthians 9:8

percentage that God asks you to. He is the provision, and we should trust Him alone. It is the most reasonable and practical thing you can do as a steward. After all, success in finance is not defined as being prosperous; it is defined as being faithful. Doing it God's way is infinitely more important than showing a profit. The principle of how you do it is more essential than what you do.

We are stewards of our time as well as our treasures. Another way to think about this is through the opportunities that are afforded to us. Opportunity doesn't knock very often, so you must seek them where they may be found. You don't make opportunities, you prepare for them, and you prepare for that which faith has revealed.[73] Many opportunities are missed because we are unprepared for them. We simply miss our chance because we did not prepare.

A good example of this was while I was pastoring in Colorado. A young man had accepted the call to preach and was preparing to go to school. The problem was that he had not heard from the school and the time was nearing when he had to go or wait until the next semester. He was in a real quandary. Should he sell his mobile home or wait until he had been accepted? He came to me for advice, and I asked him if he *knew* the Lord had called him to go to school. He was certain that He had, but they had not sent him notice of acceptance. I asked him what would happen if he did not sell his mobile home. He said he would not be able to go. I told him that if he was certain the Lord had called him to attend this school, he should prepare to go, even if he had not heard from the school. He proceeded to sell his mobile home, and by the time he had closed on its sale, he received the letter of acceptance from the school. Had he not prepared to go to school, he would have lost that opportunity.

Often you will hear people lament they don't have enough time. The truth is everyone has the same amount of time in a day – 24 hours. It's not that we are short of time, as though we only have 20 hours in our day, but that we do not use our time efficiently.

People who are able to accomplish great things share some characteristics. First, they are focused. They have a goal, and they do not allow things to distract them from reaching their goal. Second, they are organized. They have learned not to waste motion or action.

[73] Ephesians 5:16

(My Dad used to advise me, "work smarter, not harder.") Another common characteristic is efficiency, which is the result of thinking about what you are doing and practicing it repeatedly. Successful people are able to make it look easy because they have taken out the wasted motion. A fourth characteristic is diligence. They neither give up nor quit. Equally important, they do not burn themselves out. They stay with a job until it is done. Finally, they finish well. Completing a job well is a very satisfying thing. They tie up the loose ends with the three R's: restore, replace and return. They restore their tool's function by fixing what's broken and repairing what's worn. They replace what is used up and worn out. They return what is to be used again to its place.

Stewardship of talents actually deals with more than just your abilities. It also includes your person (who and what you are) and your spiritual gifts. Natural talent or ability is your capacity to do certain tasks. It is dependent upon your physique, your mental capacity, and your experience. These things limit your capacity to function. You can run only so fast, jump so high, hold your breath so long, etc. It is true that these limits can be stretched through training and development, but they are not endless. These limits define your natural talent. Not everyone can be the fastest or best. Your natural talent is something that you are born with, and it is therefore a gift from God. What you do with it and how you use it is up to you, but it defines your values. You can use it for personal gain and glory, or you can use it for the good of man and the glory of God. You only hold it for a time, and then it will be gone. How will you answer God when He requires you to give an account of its use?

Many people are dissatisfied with how God made them. They feel that they were born with an unfair handicap. They are dissatisfied with their appearance, weight, level of intelligence, family situation, or station in life. They long for what others have and are generally unhappy with who they are and what they do in life. There is a sense that they have been shortchanged, and now they suffer because of their limitations. However, there is a problem with this line of thinking. The common thread to every thought or feeling of inadequacy is that God made a mistake when he made you. We are essentially charging the righteous, holy, loving God for not being righteous or loving and for failing in His creation. But what makes us think that we have better knowledge about what is best than the all-knowing, all-powerful, righteous God? It is our self-centeredness. Instead of trusting Him, we criticize Him. Instead of believing that He has our best interest at heart, we charge Him with failure. God made you exactly how you need to be. You are exactly the right height, weight, color, ability, intelligence, and you are living in the right time. You were born to the right parents. You were born in the right state and country. You were designed "for such a time as this."[74] He has given you the unique opportunity to make a difference in a very needy world. It is only through trusting the Lord with who and what you are that you have peace in the midst of the storm around you. Our limitations are for a purpose, just as our abilities are for a purpose. This is where faith in the Lord is essential. We will be the happiest of all people and the most contented of servants when we find God's plan for our lives. Indeed, we could not be as happy if all of our so-called inadequacies were addressed. They would become a burden and interfere with our task. When God withheld, it was to bless you, and when God gave to you, it was to bless you. Do you not see the wisdom of God in making you just as you are for this time? God hasn't cheated you; rather, He has fitted you for your opportunities and choices.

And now we come to Spiritual Gifts, which are distinct from worldly gifts. These do not follow worldly rules but spiritual principles. They are supernatural in that they are beyond the natural and cannot be defined or understood by the natural world. The natural world is affected by the exercise of spiritual gifts, but it cannot understand spiritual principles. The only way a spiritual gift can be exercised is by faith. They are for the purpose of exposing, equipping, and doing the will of God. According to I Corinthians 12:7, every Christian has at least one spiritual gift. There is at least one way that you can expose God to the lost world. This is the window for the lost world to see God through the Christian and the door for the saved to enter into His presence. This is an important opportunity and responsibility. You are a steward of those opportunities, and you are to avail yourselves of every opportunity.

---

[74] Ester 4:14

Sanctification or Holiness

Another logical step of faith is sanctification or holiness. The word holy means set apart or separate.

> *I beseech you therefore, brethren, by the mercies of God, that ye present your bodies a living sacrifice, holy, acceptable unto God, which is your reasonable service.*[75]

> *Sanctify yourselves therefore, and be ye holy: for I am the Lord your God.*[76]

> *But as he which hath called you is holy, so be ye holy in all manner of conversation;*[77]

> *Because it is written, Be ye holy; for I am holy.*[78]

> *Wherefore come out from among them, and be ye separate, saith the Lord, and touch not the unclean thing; and I will receive you.*[79]

The Scriptures are very clear that Christians are to live holy lives. Perhaps one of the main reasons that people ignore God today is that Christians look and act so much like the lost. However, if you can't tell the difference, there may not be a difference. The one word that may best describe God is the word Holy. Have you noticed that people talk about what they are interested and involved in? The people of this world talk about this world; whereas the people of God talk about the spiritual world. People of this world use worldly means; however, people of God operate by faith. People of this world defend their rights, but people of God are secure in Jesus. People of this world are trying to earn a place with God, but people of God receive their place as a free gift. People of this world are takers,

---

[75] Romans 12:1

[76] Leviticus 20:7

[77] 1Peter 1:15

[78] 1Peter 1:16

[79] 2Corinthians 6:17

and the people of God are givers. On and on the contrast goes, but when you find a child of God, he stands out as different. As long as we hold on to our worldliness, we will remain ineffective and powerless. We must separate ourselves to the Lord and His ways to become all that we can be.

Transformation

A very important step of faith is transformation.

I beseech you therefore, brethren, by the mercies of God that ye present your bodies a living sacrifice, holy acceptable to God which is your reasonable service. (v.1) And be not conformed to this world: but be ye transformed by the renewing of your mind, that ye may prove what is that good, and acceptable, and perfect, will of God. (v.2) [80]

In this text we find (connected to "your reasonable service" in v.1) the instruction to be transformed in v.2. The word for transformed is the Greek word m*etamorphoo*, which means metamorphosis. Consider how dramatic it is to change from a woolly worm to a butterfly. The worm is confined to crawling, but the butterfly can soar in the heavens. The worm was given wholly to consuming food, but the butterfly is focused on the next generation. The worm is ugly, whereas the butterfly is beautiful. The worm winds up getting caught in a web of its own spinning, but the butterfly is free to travel about. The body of the worm is large, but that of the butterfly is small. This is similar to the dramatic change a Christian goes through in his faith walk. Self-interest gives up to the will of God. Worldliness is lost, and spirituality takes its place. Instead of struggling to exist, the freedom of Christ and His peace are ours. Assurance of the promises of God become certain, and the power to overcome is a fact. You don't have to live all your life crawling around in this world. You can rise above the circumstances and soar in the heavens of promise.[81]

---

[80] Romans 12:1-2
[81] See appendix 5.2

Not only are we instructed to be changed, but we are also told what to do so that the change may take place. All you need is a cocoon experience. The worm must pass through the cocoon in order to become a butterfly. It is as essential to the butterfly as it is to the spiritual man. Without it, the transformation cannot take place. I doubt the worm has any understanding of what is happening to him, but understanding is not necessary for the transformation to take place. When you consider what a cocoon is, it begins to make more sense. A cocoon is really a web that is spun by the worm, in which he is caught in the middle. All hope for the worm is lost. It will never again be what it was.

Our cocoon is really the impossible situation that we find ourselves caught in. It is something that we chose or did ourselves, compounded by numerous repetitions (much like the strands of the web) and then hardened by outside forces. It holds us fast and is uncomfortable. It is a time of great struggle. It is in this position that the Lord refashions and reshapes us. Life in the cocoon is altogether different than it was before. It is here that we begin to experience life as it shall be in the future. The only hope for the worm is to become a butterfly. It has never had instruction or training, but it does it right the first time. The only explanation is that God is involved in it.

The above verse, and many others, reveal that God is involved in our transformation and guides us through it in the person of the Holy Spirit. What I could never do, God enables me and directs me in doing it.

These changes take time just as the transformation of the worm into a butterfly takes time. We call this process *sanctification*. It begins at the point of conversion and ends at the rapture or our death. The word, sanctification means "setting apart." It means the same as the word, holy. We are being set apart from the world system unto the Lord.

The changes are internal and deal with character, value, and principles. They are what make up the man. They determine courses of action and reactions. They are based on the composition of the heart.

In addition to changing internally, we are changed externally as well. All manner of change is necessary for each of us when adjusting to living a spiritual life. We must move from the works system to the faith system in all areas of our life. It is no longer an eye for an eye, but now we learn to love our enemies. It is no longer what seemeth right unto me, but what sayeth the Lord. It is no longer *me* first, but rather doing good to all men. It is no longer getting, but giving. It is not the letter of the law but the Spirit of the law that giveth life. How disproportional a Christian appears who holds bitterness, anger, or selfishness? We will never soar in the heavens when weighted with such cares of this world. It is in the struggle that we release our grip on our old way of life and place our faith in God's way of living. The trials and difficulty of this life serve a very important purpose. They enable us to develop our wings of faith that we might soar above the sphere of the natural into the sphere of the spiritual. The restrictions and limitations of this life cause the development of our spirituality, which prepares us for eternity.

Finding your ministry

I remember being quite young when some of the older men of the church would ask me "What do you want to do when you grow up?" I would try to think of something that seemed glamorous or something they might think was good, and that is how I answered. This question did not cause me any concern until my late teens. I thought about it a lot and could not settle on any specific career. I was in good physical shape, had good eyesight and did pretty well in math and science. I was primarily interested in flying, but the military would not consider me without a college degree. I began to take different jobs, but none of them were really satisfying to me. After I had been out of school for several years, got married and began to raise a family, I was no closer to finding my niche than when I was in my late teens. It seemed that all my efforts had moved me further away from this great discovery than if I had done nothing. I have since learned that my experience was much like so many others I have met along life's journey. Some find what their life's work is at a young age. Many find it by the time they finish schooling. Still others do not find it until they stumble onto it later in life. There is a group, larger than you might guess, that never find it.

In my case, I discovered it in my mid-twenties. I wasn't looking for it specifically. I was looking for answers to life in general. By this time, I had attended two different colleges, held jobs in produce sales, orchard care and harvesting. I was a telephone installer, miner, heavy equipment operator, surveyor, laborer, carpenter and small crane operator, yet I still didn't know what I wanted to do as a career. I spent a summer traveling and later had started my family. Still, I felt lost as to my purpose. I looked in multiple churches and in various denominations to find answers. Finally, I found the answer to life: Jesus. I had stumbled over Him as the answer many times because I had never responded to Him by faith. It was by faith that I made peace with Him and became a Christian. That settled part of my search, but I still didn't know what to do about a career.

I thought it would all become clear after being saved, but it didn't. The fog didn't lift for a couple more years. My pride, prejudices, and preconceived ideas were muffling God's directions. Before God's call to me could be seriously considered, I had to deal with myself and had a lot of unlearning to do before I could build on the right principals. The Lord worked with my faith at my pace and dealt with each issue. After He humbled me, taught me and demonstrated His love to me, I was ready to listen.

I thought it was my decision as to what I would become, and that is true with one important caveat. My choice had to be fitted within the scope of His design by faith. You don't make a hammer out of a saw. We have been designed for a specific service, and when we try to operate outside of that plan, we often frustrate ourselves as well as those around us. Trying to be something we are not will bring untold problems. On the other hand, if we operate within the scope of our design by faith, we will achieve success and benefit many, resulting in a real satisfaction. The problem I had, and I think so many others have as well, was that I didn't think what God had in mind for me was worthy of my effort. I never saw myself as the best or greatest, and neither did anyone else. What I really wanted was acceptance, love and appreciation. I bought into the idea that the only way to achieve this was by being the best. I could see my flaws and knew I came up short. I failed to see that God's plan for me would bring all I longed for, but I could not acquire it for myself.

After the Lord worked with me, I was ready to do things God's way. In fact, I couldn't see any other way to proceed. My discovery was that I was exactly fitted for the task ahead. All my experiences and skills were fitted to my needs. How do you fit telephone installation, surveying, road construction, fruit and produce and a number of other jobs together into a career? God had a plan for me that included all of these and more. Looking back, I realize that His plan for me did not become apparent until much later in life. Now I can see God's wisdom for me.

God's plan for me was first to walk by faith and then to use me as a bi-vocational pastor. My first calling is to preach and teach the gospel. This is my ministry. The Lord confirmed that to me quite clearly and in such a way I would never have any doubts about it. The part that didn't become clear for a number of years was that He wanted me to minister to the small churches that didn't have the means for full support. It is really quite a unique task: a full-time position with part-time financial support. This troubled me for a long time because I thought I was lacking in faith by not trusting the Lord for full financial support. The Lord showed me I was in good company. Paul was a tentmaker in order to do the missionary work he was set apart for. Peter was a fisherman, and Jesus was a carpenter. Sometimes the Lord will ask something of an individual that may seem odd or unfair. It is important that we trust Him with these details so that we do not miss the hidden treasures. In order to serve the small church, I needed to work at a secular job. It has given me a liberty that I would have never known otherwise. It has forced me to organize far beyond what I would have done if I hadn't been forced. It has been the opportunity to touch lives that I would never have had contact with otherwise. It has given me sensitivity to the problems of the working members of the church. It has helped me with perspective and humility. These and many other blessings awaited me by submitting to God's plan, a plan that I did not understand or want.

And how does secular work fit into God's plan? As I learned to walk hand in hand with the Lord, I was lead into construction and became a project superintendent, a project manager, and even the owner of my own business. I have used things from every job I have ever done on the job site. They were all preparation for me. I used the heavy equipment operation and highway construction to envision the site work. I use the telephone installation in understanding the needs of the communication systems and making necessary preparations. I use the ornamental ironwork experience in meeting installation needs for handrails. I use the surveying experience in dealing with property lines and building locations. I use the sales experience to enhance customer relations. I use the carpenter experience in structural considerations. On and on it goes. All of the things I experience in construction and the people I meet and deal with have become a vast resource of illustration of spiritual truth.

My life now is rich and full. I have the experience of having pastored five churches, seven preachers began their ministry under my ministry, I have seven children who are all doing well, 22 grand children, and four great-grandchildren. I am still married to my wife of more than 48 years. My work has been rewarding, and I have been blessed with good health. Praise the Lord. As I look forward, I find it just as unclear as it was when I was a teen. I do not know what lies ahead, but I believe that the greatest days are ahead. Retirement for me is not having to be bi-vocational. I can devote my full energy into the one thing I am here for. It is yet to be seen what God will do with the least of the brethren.

So it is with every believer: God has a specific plan for you that will both satisfy the believer and glorify the Lord. Every believer has at least one gift and at least one ministry. "But the manifestation of the Spirit is given to every man to profit withal."[82] It is not necessary for you to know what the gift is as much as it is to be recognized by others. When others see it, they catch a glimpse of Christ in you, and the Lord is glorified.[83] Your spiritual gift(s) is any means whereby others can see the Lord in you and your actions. You may not see it for a long time, but others will and they will be brought into closer contact with their Creator, the Lord Jesus by the exercise of your gift. A spiritual gift is not given to make you feel good, for that is not its purpose. When you exercise it, you will sense more of God's presence and consequently will feel the excitement of His working. If you were to pursue the sensation, you would soon become cold

---

[82] 1Corinthians 12:7

[83] Perhaps it could be rightly said "the Lord is clarified." That is, better *known* because He is better seen.

spiritually; but by ministering to others with the gift you have been given, you will in turn be ministered unto. It is God's intent to use you in your station in life. He wants to use you in your family, in your vocation, your recreation and in your re-creation or personal time with Him. The sooner you open the way for Him to direct you, the sooner you will see Him using you.

God, in His wisdom, calls some men for the specific purpose of equipping the saints so that they can do the work of ministering.

And he gave some, apostles; and some, prophets; and some, evangelists; and some, pastors and teachers; 12 For the perfecting of the saints, for the work of the ministry, for the edifying of the body of Christ: 13 Till we all come in the unity of the faith, and of the knowledge of the Son of God, unto a perfect man, unto the measure of the stature of the fullness of Christ:[84]

The Lord does not call the men who *we* might call. He calls them that He chooses.[85] We would not see them as examples of great success in this world, but God sees them as great successes in the spiritual world. They are men specifically called and chosen and faithful.[86] They are worthy of double honor and are to be followed as they will give an account unto the Lord.

---

[84] Ephesians 4:11-13

[85] 1Corinthians 1:26-29

[86] Revelations 17:14

Chapter 6

The Potential of Faith

A man I knew from Clear Creak Baptist College was pasturing his first church after graduation. The church was young and had not built an identity or founded the principles on which it was to be established. It had struggled continually to meet its commitments and expenses, and an attitude of defeat was starting to settle into the congregation.

The pastor had studied the church budget, and for the most part, there was nothing amiss; however, when he examined the expenditures, he found that, although the church had designated 10% of its donations to mission giving, they had given nothing. When they held the next business meeting, the pastor asked the congregation about this discrepancy, and they replied it was because there wasn't anything left for missions after all the bills had been paid. The pastor quickly realized that the problem wasn't in the Lord's supply line but that there was a clog in the faith of the membership. He stated that honesty was essential in all that a church does, to which everyone agreed. He then stated that their budget should also reflect that honesty, and if they believed that it was the will of the Lord to give a certain percentage, it ought to become a priority that they meet it. He then charged the church to rethink the budget with this adjustment. He instructed them to set the mission giving at an amount they believed it should be, but that they should pay it first, even before paying the pastor. Despite much objection, the church finally decided to cut the amount to 5% of their general budget, and they agreed to pay it first, even before paying the pastor or the bills.

A pastor foregoing his salary may seem like a drastic measure, but in this situation, there were two principles at stake. The first, he had already established, and that was honesty, to which everyone had agreed. The second principle was one of faith. Would they trust in what they could see or in what the Lord had promised? What would it say to the community if they would not trust Him to care for the needs of the church? The pastor was standing on the principle of faith and not in a paycheck, so he asked the church to stand with him.

Since its inception, this church had endured a shortage of funds, but the first month after they made the change, they had collected an amount over and above their budget requirements. In fact, they didn't experience any kind of shortage for the next two years. During this time, they were able to build a new facility and had grown to twice the membership.

A month came when they had a shortage of funds, and without notifying the church, the mission funds were once again withheld to pay the pastor's salary. The pastor, however, had it settled in his heart that they were going to follow the faith principle, even if it meant that he wouldn't receive his pay. The pastor confronted the treasurer and once again insisted that they first pay the mission fund. He reluctantly did so, and in the months that followed, they were able to increase their mission giving from the original 5% up to 14% and only had a total indebtedness of less than $40K at the time he concluded his 4 ½ years of ministry there. At no time was there a month that he was not paid as their pastor.

The struggle that this church had is very common in both the individual and in the church. Not only is it commonplace, it is also necessary. The Bible speaks of this struggle in Galations 5:17. "For the flesh lusteth against the Spirit, and the Spirit against the flesh: and these are contrary the one to the other: so that ye cannot do the things that ye would."

It is not a question of God's willingness to answer our prayer or to supply our needs. Instead, it is a contest between the old nature to sin and the new nature to walk by faith.[87] We are accustomed to

---

[87] II Corinthians 10:3-6 For though we walk in the flesh, we do not war after the flesh: (For the weapons of our warfare are not carnal, but mighty through God to the pulling down of strong holds;) 5 Casting down imaginations, and every high thing that exalteth

having our own way and are not used to submitting our will to God. All faith ventures will require the power of God to accomplish and are impossible without it. Vision will not be apparent until faith is applied. If we are to become all that God has intended, we must deal with our old nature and subdue it, making it subject to the new nature in Christ. The battle is necessary for us to reject the temptation to deal with it on our own, which will certainly result in defeat. This battle will continue until a decisive victory has been won.[88] Whichever one wins determines the results of the struggle.

This struggle is only won by our faith in the Lord Jesus.[89] Try as you may, you will fail again and again in attempting the work of God by effort. This is one of the hardest lessons we will learn in our growth in faith. We recognize that others have failed us, yet we often fail to consider that we have failed ourselves even more often. The only one who is truly dependable is the Lord.

Our unbelief is simply distrust of God and His motives. God really does intend to supply our every need. Yet, our faith doesn't bring the desired result because our sin blocks His supply. We would all agree that He can, but we don't all believe that He will. We stagger in unbelief by refusing to trust God for what He has said. We are more willing to trust our perception than we are to trust God's instructions. He is the only one who has a complete perspective on how things really are. Unbelief will stop the flow of God's blessings. In the Old Testament, the children of Israel could not enter the promised land the first time because of unbelief,[90] yet it was plainly God's will for them to possess the land. In the New Testament, the disciples were unable to cast out demons because of unbelief[91] and even Jesus was unable to do some miracles because of

---

itself against the knowledge of God, and bringing into captivity every thought to the obedience of Christ.

[88] For in many things we offend all. If any man offend not in word, the same is a perfect man, and able also to bridle the whole body. James 3:2

[89] For whatsoever is born of God overcometh the world: and this is the victory that overcometh the world, even our faith. 1 John 5:4

[90] They were not able to enter in because of unbelief. Hebrews 3:9

[91] Matthew 17:14-21

the unbelief of the people.[92] Hebrews 4:11 gives us this admonition: "Let us labor therefore to enter into that rest, lest any man fall after the same example of unbelief."

Unbelief must be confronted and removed if our faith is to become effective. We simply cannot allow anything to inflate itself in any way so as to obscure our confidence and view of God. Everything must be subject to God. He is Omnipotent, which means all powerful. All power (including Satanic and dark powers) are subject to Him. No impossibility can override His power. He is also Omniscient, which means all knowing. There is no knowledge that has eluded Him, and He has considered everything. You will never surprise Him. He is Omnipresent, which means everywhere present. He will never leave you, for wherever you go, He is there. It also means that there is nothing unavailable to Him. If you have a need, He is the supply. It also includes all time. There is no place in time that He is unavailable. He is there in the good times as well as crises. He is the alpha and the omega, the beginning and the end. Finally, He is Omni-sovereign, which means the rightful owner and ruler of all creation. He has no shortages. There is nothing He lacks. When your view of God includes all these things, unbelief will no longer block your faith.

God's plan may also be blocked by the sin of apathy. It may manifest itself by either a refusal to act (you have not because you ask not) or by not valuing God's objective in preference to your own perception (your own will).[93] It has been rightly said that all that is necessary for Satan to take over the world is for righteous men to do nothing. Apathy is paralyzing and opposes faith on every point. It will certainly block God's blessings because then God has to deal with you before he can work through you. God's blessings are intended to flow continually as water does through a pipe. Sin blocks the flow and must be removed before the flow can be restored.

---

[92] And he did not many mighty works there because of their unbelief. Matthew 13:58

[93] James 4:2 Ye lust, and have not: ye kill, and desire to have, and cannot obtain: ye fight and war, yet ye have not, because ye ask not. 3 Ye ask, and receive not, because ye ask amiss, that ye may consume it upon your lusts. {lusts: or, pleasures} 4 Ye adulterers and adulteresses, know ye not that the friendship of the world is enmity with God? Whosoever therefore will be a friend of the world is the enemy of God.

I have illustrated the effect of sin on ventures of faith using unbelief and apathy. The truth is that all sin has the same effect on our faith. It blocks God's blessings, prevents our spiritual growth and destroys our lives. It is first necessary to open the supply lines to be able to receive the blessings of God. Consider what the possibilities are for those who have been confronted with their sin, confessed them and are now living in obedient faith in Christ. They are simply amazing and beyond our comprehension.[94]

The first possibility is actually a promise. The Lord will quicken our mortal bodies.[95] In Greek, the word, *quicken* means to make alive. It is in reference to the coming alive spiritually and is the product of a new birth. The believer has become the dwelling place of the eternal, living God. As such, he has been cleaned up (his sin has been fully, finally and forever paid for). He has become a product of God's specific handiwork.[96] He has become joint heirs with Christ[97] and will receive an eternal resurrected body like that of Jesus.[98], [99]

When acting in faith on God's revelation, we are able to see the unseen and do the impossible. Just the changes in our eternal body are enough to make it worthwhile to become a Christian, but these are only fundamental changes.

God's plan for us is so much greater than that. His plan for us is not just to benefit us but to use us to carry that promise to as many

---

[94] But if the Spirit of him that raised up Jesus from the dead dwell in you, he that raised up Christ from the dead shall also quicken your mortal bodies by his Spirit... Romans 8:11

[95] But as it is written, eye hath not seen, nor ear heard, neither have entered into the heart of man, the things which God hath prepared for them that love Him. I Corinthians 2:9

[96] Ephesians 2:10

[97] And if children, then heirs; heirs of God, and joint-heirs with Christ; if so be that we suffer with him, that we may be also glorified together. Romans 8:17

[98] 1 Thessalonians 4:16 For the Lord himself shall descend from heaven with a shout, with the voice of the archangel, and with the trump of God: and the dead in Christ shall rise first: 17 Then we which are alive and remain shall be caught up together with them in the clouds, to meet the Lord in the air: and so shall we ever be with the Lord.

[99] Beloved, now are we the sons of God, and it doth not yet appear what we shall be: but we know that, when he shall appear, we shall be like him; for we shall see him as he is. John 3:2

as will accept it. He has given us the ministry of reconciliation.[100] God's intention is not only to bless us with His presence but to also make us a part of His working. We are to be tools in His hand to accomplish His task here on earth. We are promised everything we need to accomplish this task.[101] The possibilities are limitless. He will do whatever you need or ask within the confines of faith in Christ and the will of God. This power is not for our consumption but for the furtherance of the kingdom of Christ. When we walk by faith in Christ, we become the extension of His hands and feet. That is why when we have done it to the least of the brethren, we have done it to Christ.

God's plan for us extends beyond the quickening and beyond spiritual service to include reigning with Him. The Bible does not define the extent of this reign, but it does give us several applications. The first was the authority to bind and loose.[102] Notice that this authority was not given for the will of man but in attempt to redeem the brother and to do the will of God. Nor was it given to a single individual but to the church, for offences come to all. It was not given because Peter was anyone special, for Jesus declared that flesh and blood had not brought the revelation. Jesus was commending the faith that Peter exercised, which caused his revelation of who Christ is. Only moments later we see Peter acting in the strength of the flesh, and the Lord soundly rebuked him.

Secondly, we find that to those who overcome the false teaching of Satan is promised power over nations.[103] We know that when Christ returns to the earth at the end of the Great Tribulations, He will bring His saints with Him and set up His earthly kingdom, reigning here for a thousand years.[104] Though this reign begins through the

---

[100] And all things are of God, who hath reconciled us to himself by Jesus Christ, and hath given to us the ministry of reconciliation. 2 Corinthians 5:18

[101] See Appendix 6.1

[102] Verily I say unto you, Whatsoever ye shall bind on earth shall be bound in heaven: and whatsoever ye shall loose on earth shall be loosed in heaven. Matthew 18:18

[103] And he that overcometh, and keepeth my works unto the end, to him will I give power over the nations: Revelation 2:26

[104] Blessed and holy is he that hath part in the first resurrection: on such the second death hath no power, but they shall be priests of God and of Christ, and shall reign with him a thousand years. Revelation 20:6

church, it will extend beyond our death through the 1000-year reign of Christ.

Thirdly, we are told that we will judge the world and even judge angles.[105] A third of the angles of heaven were cast out of heaven when Satan tried to overthrow God, and they have been kept in chains in darkness unto judgment.[106] It may be that we will participate in that judgment.

And finally, God's plan for us is eternal. It is not riding on a cloud, playing a harp. We are to be the dwelling place of God, Himself. We are His tent of dwelling, or tabernacle. Our bodies are the temple of God. Our potential is constrained to living a life of faith in this temporal world, and that life will extend on through eternity. It will not only affect things in time but also for eternity.

---

[105] Do ye not know that the saints shall judge the world? and if the world shall be judged by you, are ye unworthy to judge the smallest matters? 1 Corinthians 6:2 Know ye not that we shall judge angels? how much more things that pertain to this life? 1 Corinthians 6:3

[106] And the angels which kept not their first estate, but left their own habitation, he hath reserved in everlasting chains under darkness unto the judgment of the great day. Jude 1:6

Chapter 7

The Trial of Faith

That the trial of your faith, being much more precious than of gold that perisheth, though it be tried with fire, might be found unto praise and honor and glory at the appearing of Jesus Christ.

– I Peter 1:7

During the spring of 2012, I began experiencing intense pain in my left knee. The pain was bad enough that it made walking difficult. My wife and I were going to be taking a trip to Niagara Falls in the coming weeks, and I didn't want walking to be a problem, so I resolved to see a doctor. At the office, the doctor examined my knee and said that she wanted me to get an MRI.

A few days before, I had discovered a lump on the side of my neck, just below my left ear. It was sore, but it didn't cause me concern, as it was not uncommon for me to have swollen glands. But since I was already there, and since the doctor had asked if there was anything else I wanted to talk about, I went ahead and mentioned the lump in my neck. After she examined me, she said that she wanted me to have an MRI on my neck, as well. She seemed quite serious, which caused me some concern. So I asked if she suspected cancer. She said that she did, and in that brief moment, my whole life made a sudden turn.

When the doctor saw the results of my MRI the next day, she contacted me immediately. The report was that I had a tumor on my neck and another possible tumor on the back of my tongue. A PET scan not only later confirmed that I had two malignant tumors but that it was also stage-four cancer. They said that I would need to have surgery, which would be followed by chemotherapy and radiation treatment.

It may seem strange, but the idea of undergoing radiation and chemotherapy didn't bother me near as much as having surgery. True, the radiation treatment would cause my hair to fall out, but I didn't have much hair left to begin with. It's also true that chemo-therapy can cause a great deal of sickness, but because my hearing was already impaired somewhat, the specialist decided to use a protein-based (instead of a drug-based) treatment, which reduced the amount of sickness I would have normally had to endure. The surgical treatment was another story altogether. They said that they would need to remove a portion of my neck and my tongue, and as a result, I would be disfigured, and it would affect my ability to speak. Needless to say, this caused my wife and I a great deal of concern.

When the radiologist examined me, however, she informed me that surgery would be unnecessary, and this came as good news in the midst of everything else we were learning about my condition. Radiation and chemotherapy were unavoidable, however, and I would have to start treatment immediately. The next week I received a double dose of chemotherapy, followed once a week by a single dose for 7 weeks. I also began radiation treatments once a day for five days a week until I completed 31 treatments.

During this time, I never took any pain medication, never got sick, never lost my energy level, and kept most of what little hair I had before they even discovered the cancer. I lost 55 pounds, but this was much needed, as I was a little overweight. I was on a feeding tube for about half of the treatment time, but I responded very well, and the medical team marveled that I began healing so quickly. Since completing all of my treatments, I have been cancer free, and with all the changes my body has undergone, my original problem –my knee—quit hurting some time during the whole process, for reasons unknown to me.

Sometimes people wonder why God allows bad things to happen to them when, at the same time, God loves them. The truth is that, it is precisely God's love that permits such challenges and obstacles. What we face, endure, and finally overcome is for only a moment, but the lessons we learn are for an eternity. I felt from the beginning that the Lord had allowed me to face cancer as an opportunity for others to see Him at work. My wife and I chose to face each day as an opportunity to reveal God through this experience. I accepted the fact that I would have to endure a lot and that it could even end my life. My greatest concern was neither of these things but whether I would properly represent my Lord in the midst of this trial. I believed that I had been entrusted with a great opportunity, and I did not want to fail. I remembered what the apostle Paul wrote in I Thessalonians. 4:13, "that ye sorrow not, even as others which have no hope." Then I thought about I Peter 4:12-13

Beloved, think it not strange concerning the fiery trial which is to try you, as though some strange thing happened unto you: But rejoice, inasmuch as ye are partakers of Christ's sufferings; that, when his glory shall be revealed, ye may be glad also with exceeding joy.

I also acknowledged Romans 8:28 that "all things work together for good," and I recalled the oft quoted phrase: *if God brings you to it, He will bring you through it.* I believed all of it, and so I stood on His promise. I sent out a weekly report on what I was going through, and I began to hear from several people about how meaningful these e-mails were. I was able to preach two services at an out-of-state church that had been praying for me. I was put on multiple prayer lists. People from several states and countries around the world prayed for me. It touched me deeply and was a great encouragement. These and many other blessings are mine. If my trial can help others know God, if they can be an encouragement, if they can expose God, I am up for it, and I can trust my Lord for even greater things.

The word "trial" has two purposes. The first is for the purpose of exposing a weakness or flaw. That is not the purpose that is used in the above verse. The purpose is to prove or demonstrate its ability. Engineers use a "load test" to see if a beam or a specific construction would in fact do what it was designed to do. If it could carry the load of its design, it passed the test. They are not so interested in finding out the limit of its ability but whether it would handle the load for which it was designed. It was for the purpose of approval rather than finding fault, and so it is with God. He is not looking for us to fail but to succeed.

There are at least six reasons why God would put your faith to the test:

> We need to learn how to trust God
> We need to know who we really are
> The world needs to see faith in the Lord really work
> We need to be strengthened for battle
> We need the encouragement of victories
> We must discover our eternal reality

Each one would be enough reason by itself, but God has much more in mind for the Christian.

We need to learn how to trust God

There is no better way to learn than on the job training. It is in the exercise of the experience that we truly learn. We also learn from our successes and our failures. Our successes help us to learn what works, and our failures teach us why something doesn't work, as well as the consequences of why it doesn't work. Why do those who are in the wrong prosper while those who walk straight have so many problems? The idea of having our faith put to the test is very foreign in a world where deeds, comforts and power are the norm. The Bible has the answer, and it makes a lot of sense when understood. John 8:38 – 44 explains that the worldly are being trained by their father, and the saved are being trained by their Father. This world is not all there is to life. Just as a growing child is prepared for adult life by carrying certain responsibilities, like picking up his toys, the trials of life itself are preparation for eternity.

We need to know who we really are

The strength of your faith in God is evidenced in the choices you make under stress. *To thine own self, be true*. It has been said that you don't really know a person until you see them function under stress. I think it is also true that you do not really know yourself until you face the trials of life. That is what the entire book of Job is all about. A righteous man is bombarded with stress beyond measure in losing his family, fortune, fame, friends and fitness, for no apparent reason. In all of this he declares, "Though He slay me, yet will I trust Him." The book closes with Job being restored double for everything he lost.

All too often we see Christians quitting when the going gets rough. The trumpet gives an uncertain sound and creates confusion about God coming through. People are looking for a faith that produces the quality of life that agrees with the Bible. It is not so much of what you say, but what you are that makes the difference to them. Does your life properly reflect the image of God? I have found that most lost people are looking for a relationship with God that will overcome these types of events, which are common to man. If what I offer isn't in step with that, I will fail to even gain an audience.

The world needs to see that faith in the Lord really works

"Let your light so shine before men, that they may see your good works, and glorify your Father which is in heaven."[107]

Those who are lost look at the lives of those who profess a faith in Jesus as Lord of their lives. If they fail to see faith working for the believers, they will conclude that there is no difference and will reject The Truth of the Gospel as a lie. Our *faith* will be either a light to show the path or a shroud that hides the way to God. We need to know that we are part of the solution and not part of the problem. The world is in a state of confusion and chaos. One of the great questions of today is how to cope? The world offers a flood of answers that offer no lasting solutions because they are based on everything but the Lord. The Bible does not teach us to be escape artists ("He will make a way of escape"[108]), but it teaches us to be overcomers.[109] ("For whatsoever is born of God overcometh the world: and this is the

---

[107] Matthew 5: 16

[108] I Corinthians 10:13

[109] 1 John 5:4

victory that overcometh the world, even our faith."[110]). The escape referenced above is not from trials but from temptation. God is not trying to make our journey free from struggles but free from sin. If the world can see our faith in Christ working for us in that we have victory in this world, they will flock to our doors to get the same thing for themselves. Christians also need to see examples of strong faith. Without it, they will not understand the message of the gospel of Christ as to victory over circumstances, emotions, evil men, and satanic forces in this world.

We need to be strengthened for battle

The church of today is weak and anemic. Our members are tossed to and fro with every wind of doctrine. We often refuse to practice certain teachings of the Bible while at other times we practice that which is not sound doctrine. We vote our desires rather than that of the Lord. We elect leadership by popularity rather than qualification. We call pastors based on scholarship and worldly measures of success rather than spiritual maturity. We sit by and remain quiet to injustices rather than get involved and make our voices heard. We fight among ourselves but do not fight the enemy. The rulers of darkness go unchecked and wreak havoc with the church and with the lost. They grow in their power to control and in their ambitions. They pit us against ourselves and spread false doctrine and confusion. We are tossed to and fro with every new church fad and program. *It seemeth right unto me* sounds Biblical, but it isn't and opens the door to all manner of compromise. We are a people who do not have a strong foundation for what we believe and why. We need the testing to *harden our metal* and make us what we ought to be. "But speaking the truth in love, may grow up into him in all things, which is the head, even Christ."[111] Just as metal is hardened by trial (heat then cold), we need to accept the trials we face at Jesus' hand to strengthen us. We need difficulty and adversity to cause us to resist the Devil, to flee temptation, and trust the Lord. Trials work much like a cattle prod to move the cow against her own will; so also do trials cause us to act. It has been said that the greatest

---

[110] Romans 12:21

[111] Ephesians 4:15

problem in the church is apathy. The church has been the fiber for conscience and action in bygone days but is in danger of letting the nation fall to the forces of the world. Failure to properly diagnose the problem has resulted in untold loss of effort, materials, time, and lives. Unless we awaken from our slumber and be the force we can be, we may lose our nation as we know it.

We need the encouragement of victories

Another reason for the trial of our faith is that God is encouraging us along our way. The intended purpose for our testing is to prove that our faith will pass the test. It is not to find the limit, but to demonstrate that the limit has been exceeded. This is what God is revealing in the lives of the people of faith. His purpose is for us to see that our faith in Him is more than enough to overcome the trial of loss, need, comfort, or crises. It is not my faith that makes the difference, but He who my faith is in. His invitation to us is to "taste and see that the Lord is good."[112] Malachi 3:10 offers another reason:

> *...prove me now herewith, saith the Lord of hosts, if I will not open you the windows of heaven, and pour you out a blessing, that there shall not be room enough to receive it.*

We are concerned that someone might see us struggling and thereby reject our witness. The truth is, if they do not see us struggle with the same issues of life they face, and see God bigger than the problem, they will reject our God, which is the greater need. It is not we who are on trial here; it is our God. The lost world needs to see Christians in conflict and overcoming their trials by their faith in Jesus. Then they too will have hope.

We must discover our eternal reality

There is another reason for the need of having our faith tried. That is of the eternal spiritual difference it makes. "Therefore if any man be in Christ, he is a new creature: old things are passed away; behold all things are become new."[113] This verse teaches us that when

---

[112] Psalms 34:8

[113] 2 Corinthians 5:17

we become a Christian, we are the new creation of God, and our lives will never be the same. Our sin (past, present and future) has once and for all-time been paid for. Our lives are guaranteed to bring us to the throne fully justified. The Holy Spirit of God indwells us from that point forward, for all time, and will never leave us. All events in our lives have purpose. Nothing can touch us that has not been allowed by the Lord. These are established facts at the moment of salvation.

Then we come to the caution of the Apostle Paul to take heed in how we build on this foundation.

> *According to the grace of God which is given unto me, as a wise master builder, I have laid the foundation, and another buildeth thereon. But let every man take heed how he buildeth thereupon.*[114]

When we stand before the Lord and He judges our lives, the only things that will be salvageable will be those expressions of faith in Him. They are valuable to Him. He wants to parade our faith in heaven. Our works, on the other hand, will be tried by fire.[115] The foundation or object of faith is Jesus Christ (v. 11). There are three types of works that are easily gathered but have a low value and will not stand the test of fire, (wood, hay and stubble or straw). These can be understood as carnal or worldly purposes. Then there are three types of works that are hard to accumulate, have a high value, and will stand the test of fire. In fact, the purpose of the fire is to purify them and make them even more valuable. These can be understood as spiritual purposes and are eternal in their nature. The caution is that we should be very selective in what types of works we do: either works of flesh or works of faith. Only those works of faith will remain after the test of fire, for they are eternally valuable.

Someone who understood this difference is Joni Eareckson Tada. She became a paraplegic because of a swimming accident at 17 years of age. Instead of becoming reactive to the situation, she choose to use it as a gift from God, and for 43 years she has been a

---

[114] 1 Corinthians 3:10

[115] I Corinthians 3:11-15

lighthouse to many who have faced their own trials. She learned to draw with a pencil in her mouth because she couldn't use her hands. She sings beautifully and has several recordings. She has a radio ministry that reaches thousands. She started a wheel chair ministry and provides wheelchairs for those who can not afford one on their own. Besides all of the ways that the Lord is using her, she is a pleasant person to be around and encourages those around her. Her witness is a clear reflection of the Lord. She has chosen to build her life on the goodness of God, and it reveals Him.

Chapter 8

The Fight of Faith–Prerequisites

*Fight the good fight of faith, lay hold on eternal life, where-
unto thou art also called, and hast professed a good profession before many witnesses.*

– I Timothy 6:12

While I was attending Clear Creek Baptist College, we were
required to be involved in some type of ministry along
with our regular course load. At one time, I was involved in what
was known as the jail ministry, which met at a local transfer point
for prisoners who were being moved from one detention center
to another. The common area where I met with the prisoners was
surrounded by a walkway four-feet wide. Steel bars ran from the
floor to the ceiling and divided the room into two areas. The bars
were about an inch in diameter and were separated by 3 or 4 inches.
Within the common area was a row of individual cells that were also
separated by heavy steel bars.

When we entered the walkway, the prisoners would gather around
the separation and visit with us. We would talk about whatever was
on their minds and try to answer their questions. Most of the time,
the prisoners welcomed us and were respectful, but this occasion
was different. As I entered the area, I sensed an unusual tension in
the air, and everyone seemed nervous. I noticed one man who stood
at about six-feet six-inches and weighed around 300 pounds. He was

built like a body builder, and he was standing with his back to me at his cell with his hands on the bars.

As I began to talk with the first individual, I mentioned the name Jesus. Just then, this giant of a man spun on his heels and charged at me, cursing everything that was holy. The other prisoners in the common area parted like the red sea to avoid him. Instinctively, I backed up against the cinderblock wall behind me, hoping that was far enough to be safe. He hit the separating bars so hard that I wondered if he had hurt himself. He was reaching through and clawing the air just inches from me. I was so shocked at his reaction that I just stood there, flattened against the wall, speechless. There I stood for an hour listening to the greatest outpouring of vile I have ever heard, all the while being called every derogatory and demeaning name I could imagine. The other prisoners just sat in silence, keeping a safe distance. When it came time for us to leave, the guards came back to get us, and this huge man finally returned to his cell. I left feeling so low that I was unable to respond or stand up for what I believed.

I remained in shock all the next week. I couldn't study or even pray. Somewhere in the week I managed to get out a short prayer. *Lord, if that is how you are going to defend your servants, I am not going back.* I remained in shock all week and just couldn't catch my balance. Then on Sunday, just before the week was out, the Lord gently spoke to my heart.

It is time for the jail ministry.

I told you I wasn't going! I reacted to Him without thinking whom I was speaking to. Then, very patiently and gently, he spoke to me again.

Would you go again…for Me?

I struggled with that for several moments. Was I willing to endure another helping of abuse for Him? What does that say about me? Would it be any different? My mind was so full of the unknown. Finally, I said I would go and had resigned to accept whatever happened. At least I obeyed.

When we got to the jail, the dread of going back to that same cellblock became overwhelming. I wanted to panic and run. I began to climb the stairs to the second floor, and by the time I reached the top, I had resigned to face whatever was coming. As the guard opened the door to the middle cellblock, a hush fell across the room. The guard shut the door behind me, and I fastened my eyes on this giant of a man who was standing in exactly the same way as he had the week before. Everyone remained motionless and quiet. This huge man just stood there with his back to me. I watched him for what seemed like several minutes. Finally, he spun on his heals and again charged the bars where I was standing. But just before he reached the bars of separation, he fell on his knees before me, and in the same booming voice that he had cursed God, he began to apologize and beg for forgiveness. At that moment, the conviction of the Holy Spirit fell on all who were present, and I witnessed a sight that I had never seen before. Hardened criminals were falling on the floor pleading for mercy. Some were asking how they could be saved. Others were praying and confessing their sins. For an hour, I stood there beholding God's hand at work and helping those I could, feeling awestruck.

When I left this time, I was in a different kind of shock, and once again I struggled throughout the week. But this time, it was for a different reason. I couldn't figure out what had happened. I didn't talk with anyone about it, and I still couldn't pray or study my Bible.

Then on Sunday of the following week, the Lord spoke just two words. *It's time.* I didn't talk to anyone on the way to the jail, and once again, I had no idea what was in store. Still stunned by the two previous weeks, I quietly made my way up the stairs to the middle cellblock. As the guard began to unlock the door, I heard someone say from the inside, "He's back again!" As the door swung open and I walked in, the power of the Holy Spirit fell on us as it had the previous week. But this time, it was even more powerful than before. The huge man was gone, and no one remained untouched. I was working with three and four men at once. Several made professions of faith. They rededicated their lives and wanted to get right with God. Some wanted to make restitution for their crimes. Others were concerned with their family relationships. This went on for an hour, and when the guards came for us to leave, no one wanted it to end. When I left that day, I felt much different than I had the two previous weeks. God had demonstrated what happens when conflict and crises is met with faith in the Lord.

The Lord has a marvelous plan of deliverance that defeats our enemies, and at the same time completes His work in us. This underlying principle of warfare for the Christian is faith in the Lord Jesus. In order to accomplish this work, He has given us everything that is needed to fight these battles – the Holy Spirit. It is only natural to assume that we should fight with all our strength, but that is wrong. God does not ask us to use our strength, but His. Our strength is just not enough to fight spiritual battles. Satan easily overcomes those who battle in their own strength because his power is so much greater than ours. He is not constrained by physical limitations, and he has resources that far exceed ours. It is no contest when we attempt to battle with Satan on our own. The Lord's plan, however, requires nothing on our part but to believe what the Holy Spirit has revealed to us. It does not require great effort but great faith. Spiritual warfare is a joint venture between God and man, in which God is dominant and man is subordinate. The will and power are of God, and the faith is of man. What cannot be done without God cannot be stopped when we walk with Him. Satan is a created being and is not on par with God. He is outnumbered and out gunned when God's plan is implemented. That is why Jesus said, "If thou canst believe, all things are possible."[116]

It has been wisely stated that we should choose our battles carefully. This is no less true for the Christian. We get caught up in any number of battles that are neither necessary nor the will of God. Some are good causes but are of lesser importance than others. Some are of high importance but are not winnable, or it is not the right time to fight. However, there are a few battles that are important, winnable and necessary. These are the battles that should command our attention and response.

The *fight of faith* is the struggle between the 1) carnal man, 2) sin and its effect and 3) Satan and his powers verses the believer backed by the power and will of God. The Greek word for fight is *agonizomai*,[117] which is where the word *agonize* comes from. In the noun

---

[116] Mark 9:23

[117] Gonizomai, ag-o-nid'-zom-ahee–to struggle, literally (to compete for a prize), figuratively (to contend with an adversary), or genitive case (to endeavor to accomplish something):—fight, labor fervently, strive.

form, it refers to a contest, a course, struggle, or battle. The verb form means to contend or fight, as in an athletic game for a prize. This *fight of faith* is in the present tense imperative, with continuous action, which suggests that this fight is mandatory, current and to be fought to its end.

We need to identify the enemy, and in doing so, we must understand that the battle is not with any person. "For we wrestle not against flesh and blood, but against principalities, against powers, against the rulers of the darkness of this world, against spiritual wickedness in high places."[118] In other words, the battle is not physical but spiritual. It is with the lifestyle of self-indulgence.[119] Fight over principles not personalities. Fight over Doctrine not digression. Fight over error not emotion. We must stand by faith, we must stand on truth, and we must stand on the Bible.

Our battle is also with the systems that use people up, that take advantage of individuals and deprive them of what they are entitled to or have earned. Again the system will either build the individual or tear him down.

Our battle is also against the ideology of the carnal forces that are in opposition of everything that is holy, right, and good. This is the ideology that says to destroy everything that holds back the desires of man, the ideology that promotes self-interest above morality, that destroys personal rights through the letter of the law, that preserves animal life above human life, or that argues for the successful to forfeit to the lazy. When it is too much trouble to fight for the just, you yield to the collapse of a righteous governmental system. And chaos will soon follow.

Our battle is also against the satanic realm and includes all the mystical and spiritual forces of darkness. This includes forces that many believe are innocuous, such as Ouija boards, horoscopes, astrology, séances, palm reading, as well as the dark mystical forces, such as witchcraft, mediums, or Satan worship – all set to destroy everything that is good. Make no mistake about it: Satan is real, and demon possession is a reality. Do not leave a crack open for Satan

---

[118] Ephesians 6:12

[119] Really there are only two lifestyles: The self indulgent and that of faith in God.

to move into your life. Such things are no joke and ruin many lives. This is the battlefield where we are to fight.

It takes discipline, focus and skill to fight in this spiritual conflict. Once a person has begun the journey with the Lord by becoming a believer in Christ, Satan begins to throw roadblocks in his way. One of his tricks is to simply steer us off course.

Discipline

It takes discipline to avoid skirmishes that use up our resources and energies and leave us weakened in the fight of faith. A true believer possesses the Holy Spirit who will resist going in the wrong direction. Learning to listen to Him and obeying Him is a critical discipline if the believer is to be victorious. Another area of discipline is in the continual feeding of the new nature. When a believer is untaught, untrained or lazy in his studying of the scriptures, he becomes confused or bullied by circumstances and is ineffective in his warfare. If the Holy Spirit is not active in course corrections when the course is wrong, the individual does not possess the Holy Spirit and is not a believer.

There are at least five areas where we are especially susceptible to heading off on a tangent and must therefore exercise discipline. All of these are found in the book of I Timothy. The first is I Timothy 1:4-6 "and some having swerved have turned aside unto vain jangling . . ." The words, "having swerved" mean to veer off or miss the mark, to be sidetracked. This is exactly what happens when we resort to shortcuts.

These shortcuts can be grouped into three types, the first of which is false doctrine. This group includes such things as superstition, false religions and satanic influence. Superstition is most commonly understood as any belief or attitude, based on fear or ignorance, that is inconsistent with the known laws of science or with what is generally considered in the particular society as true and rational.[120] When you depart from sound doctrine or scriptural teaching, the only thing left is Satan's doctrine. King Saul tried it in I Samuel 28 when he could not get an answer from God. His impatience and

---

[120] Webster's New World Dictionary, Second Edition, Copyright 1970, The World Publishing Company

self will is what cost him the position as king as well as his life. It is very popular today to do the same thing as Saul. Psychic readings and magic are more popular today than ever before. Kids are experimenting with séances and witchcraft. False religions are springing up everywhere.

The second type of shortcut is fables and genealogies. The Greek word for fables is *"Muthos"* from which we get the word myths. The idea for genealogies is "the making of a pedigree or theories of origin."[121] One example of this is the well-known quote, "God helps those who help themselves." Several times I have been asked where this quote found in the Bible. The answer, of course, is that it's not there. It is actually a quote from Benjamin Franklin's, *Poor Richard's Almanac*. It almost sounds good enough to be a quote from the Bible, but God never said it. A second example is the theory of evolution. Let me emphatically state that it is only a theory. It is not proven, though it is taught as a fact. Some hold evolution as proof that God doesn't exist. Its premise is the justification of abortion, infanticide and social injustice. Though all who support evolution do not agree with such extremes, you can see that what you believe does make a difference. The Bible directs us to not give heed to such teachings but to heed that which leads to godly edifying.

The third type of shortcut is *vain jangling*[122] or empty noise, that which has no basis whatsoever and is just a wild guess. The Scripture points out that one of the reasons someone would make such assertions is that they desire to be teachers of the law. The desire to be noticed causes people to do extreme things. For example, look at the fans at a football game.

There are many shortcuts that are popular today. In an effort to win rather than earn, we have gambling, games and crime. In an effort to control rather than lead, we have intimidation, bullying and legalism. In an effort to seek pleasure rather than responsibility, we have cheep sex, low morals and emotional thrills. Like Esau who sold his birthright for a bowl of stew, we have a hard time seeing past the moment to the consequences of our choices. It is just as Jesus said, "Broad is the road to destruction, but straight is the gate

[121] Strong's Exhaustive Concordance of the Bible, Copyright 1980, 26th printing
[122] I Timothy 1:6

and narrow is the way that leadeth to life everlasting." Shortcuts lead to belief that has no foundation and are the result of taking the easy way out. Proverbs warns us about trusting the quick fix. "There is a way which seemeth right unto a man, but the end thereof are the ways of death."[123] We must be careful that our faith has a sure foundation. It has been rightly said that *rivers and men become crooked by taking the easy way*. Fight this error by solid Biblical doctrine. Don't give in to popular fads. Stand on the tried and true.

The second tangent that we may be diverted to is found in I Timothy 1:18-20 "which some having put away concerning faith have made shipwreck . . ." The phrase "putting away" means throw away, thrust away, or discard. The heart of apostatism is rebellion and rejection. It is the picture of a project begun, and after much effort and expense, the project is discarded as trash. It describes quitters and those changing horses in the middle of the stream. Jesus said of them, "No man putting his hand to the plow, and looking back is fit for the kingdom of God." Rebellion and rejection is common in today's world. It is so contrary to the old nature to humble ourselves because our pride and self reliance is so strong.

> *But it is happened unto them according to the true proverb, the dog is turned to his own vomit again; and the sow that was washed, to her wallowing in the mire.*[124]

Our church rolls are full of examples of those who began with the best of intentions and sincerity but have dropped out of church entirely and have even moved to a point of embitterment against God. This is because the instruction they received from the Bible was only heard but was not mixed with faith in the Lord, which brings about the new birth. Without the surrender of the will, which is in rebellion to God, a faith walk is impossible.

---

[123] Proverbs 14:12

[124] I Peter 2:21-22

No man can serve two masters: for either he will hate the one, and love the other; or else he will hold to the one, and despise the other. Ye cannot serve God and mammon.[125]

For by grace are ye saved and that not of yourselves, it is the gift of God, not of works lest any man should boast. For we are His workmanship created in Christ Jesus unto good works.[126]

Until we get past this idea that walking by faith requires our effort, we will not accept life as a gift. The problem is within mankind who has a fallen nature of sin and is totally untrustworthy. God has made provision for sin, but natural man does not know God and cannot know the things of God until he has been transformed by the new birth. Once the new birth has taken place, the Holy Spirit is permanently sealed in the believer, and He will then guide the believer in his walk. If there is no indwelling of the Holy Spirit, the new birth has not taken place, and the person is still lost.

False professions of faith are common in our churches today. Phrases like "all you have to do is ask Jesus into your heart" have done untold damage, as it leaves out repentance of sin. The requirement for salvation is repentance of sin[127] and faith in Jesus as Lord of life.[128] These are not two separate acts, even though they may be examined separately. It is one act of repenting and believing. Just as a coin has heads and tails, it is still only one coin. If there is no repenting of sin, there can be no faith in Jesus, and if there is no submission to the Lordship of Jesus, there is no repentance of sin. They go together and are two perspectives of one act. False professions occur when the doctrine of salvation is not correct or complete. When the doctrine of salvation is incorrectly taught, even a believer may question their salvation. It may take the Holy Spirit some time to teach the believer before they can have a real peace about their standing with God.

---

[125] Matthew 6:24

[126] Ephesians 2:8-10

[127] See Appendix 8.1

[128] See Appendix 8.2

The third tangent that we are apt to leave faith for is seen in I Timothy 4:1 "and some shall depart from the faith . . ." Spiritualism is any supernatural approach to God through any avenue other than the way He provided through His Son, Jesus. The word, depart means to apostatize, to cause to leave, to revolt or desert. Spiritualism is like apostatism in that it is a rejection of truth but also includes the powers of darkness and diversions from the truth. It is the practice of cults to prey on weak, inexperienced believers, leading them away from a faith walk with Jesus to a life directed by some system of legalism. The power behind this system is demonic and generally follows some combination of demons, doctrines of devils and deception.

Many people are looking for something spiritual to convince them to follow a practice. Satan is real and has many fallen angels that we know of as demons who will gladly supply a supernatural support to any error we will follow. This ranges from spiritual experiences to demon possession. The problem is that it is the seducing spirits of demons that lead in this error and not the Holy Spirit of God. Just because it is spiritual does not make it from God. It is also important to note that, although a Christian can be influenced by demons, she cannot be possessed by a demonic spirit.

The doctrines of devils would include any and all of those teachings that allow an avenue to God without requiring you to go through the door, which is Jesus. He said, "He that entereth not by the door into the sheepfold, but climbeth up some other way, the same is a thief and a robber." These doctrines come in many forms, but some of the more popular ones are psychic readings, mystics, séances astrology, horoscopes, witchcraft, Satan worship and cults.

Cults will often support their position by simply declaring their authority and then challenging the authority of the church. There are all manner of religious groups claiming they are the true church. One of their chief tools is a proof text. Their claim is to have special insight, even though a careful study of the passages they use will not support their conclusions. A third group of easily deceived individuals is those who trust no one but themselves. They make all the decisions and usually have a fear of being led astray or arrogance that they cannot be deceived. Their chief authority is their experience. Quite often you will run into these doctrines in printed form. They promise something that appeals to the natural man as an alternate to repentance of sin and faith in Jesus as Lord of life. To fight this diversion you will need a disciplined life with a continual infilling of God's spirit and study of the scriptures.

A fourth tangent the fight of faith contends with is found in I Timothy 6:10 " some coveted after . . ." The word covet means to fix the desire upon, to focus upon. It is a powerful desire that can blind us from everything else, including reason, people, advice and other values we hold normally. Gold Fever is a good example. We live in the most materialistic society that has ever existed. It is not wrong to have a lot of materialistic things; it is wrong to lust after those things. It is the love of money that is the root of all kinds of evil.[129] We believe we will know how to use money if we can just obtain it, but the Lord requires us to use what He has already given us by the principles that He has already given, and then He will trust us with more. This seems backwards, but that is how it works. Jacob first had to wrestle with the angel before reconciliation with his brother was possible. The change outwardly always follows the inward change. You have to put it in your heart before God puts it in your hand.

Of all that Satan offers, material items are basic to the carnal man. They appeal to our physical senses. They are in agreement with a physical reality. They are basic to our economy, and they appeal to the natural greed of man. It was one of the three things offered to Eve in the Garden of Eden (pleasant to the eyes); it was one of the three things Satan offered to Jesus (all of the kingdoms of the world), even though Satan wasn't the owner, and possessions are one of the three things that John stated was of the world.[130]

It should be noted that possessions are temporary. The question was asked about a multimillionaire when he died, "How much did he leave?" The answer: "All of it." You can't take it with you when you go. Jesus asked the question, "What does it profit a man if he gain the whole world and lose his own soul?" Money is simply a tool or a medium of exchange. It does not improve someone because he

---

[129] I Timothy 6:10
[130] I John 2:16

has it, nor does it diminish a man because he does not have it. With ownership comes the responsibility of care and preservation, which can rule a person's life. Its use will define a person's values and can become either a blessing or a curse. It will either make you more of a consumer or develop you as a giver. The choice is up to you. It will limit your values to earthly treasure or teach you of eternal treasure. To seek the things of the world will make you the enemy of Christ. To use the things that are in your stewardship for others will enable you to serve Christ. Don't miss it at this point, or you will veer off on a tangent that will take you far from Christ. Faith in the Lord for provision of life is the remedy.

The fifth tangent in the fight of faith is seen in 1 Timothy 6:20-21:

O Timothy, keep that which is committed to thy trust, avoiding profane and vain babblings, and oppositions of science falsely so called: {science: Gr. knowledge} 21 Which some professing have erred concerning the faith. Grace be with thee.

The word professing means to announce, or profess with misinformation, producing error or deviation from truth. Pride and arrogance are dominating characteristics of humanism. This professing will be typified with statements or declarations that are based on human (worldly) values and are contradictory to what has already been established as truth. It challenges the established principles and is unreasonable. Another of its characteristics is ridicule and demeaning of those who oppose it. It limits the argument to just the physical and knows nothing of the spiritual. Another characteristic is relativism. Relativism is the concept that points of view have no absolute truth or validity, having only relative, subjective value according to differences in perception and consideration. Today, Humanism has evolved into the position that God does not exist or that man is God. It is the result of a progression of rejections of truth and inconsistencies. To hold this position would be a total rejection of a life of faith.

The discipline to avoid these five tangents, or tricks of the Devil, require us to have complete trust in the Lord and to follow Him by faith. The first trap of Satan is to get us off course with distractions. To stay on course we will need to make course corrections. This is done by realigning ourselves to our destination by establishing and maintaining priorities, such as continual feeding on God's word and listening to the Holy Spirit. The second trap of Satan is to appeal to our sense of independence, which is really pride. This trap is avoided by humility and submission to the doctrine of the Bible. The third trap of Satan is bullying and fear. He insists that he has the power over us, and we are to conform to his way. This is nullified by our love for Jesus and our dependence on Him alone. Satan's fourth trap is distortion. That is, the idea that this world is all that there is. He would like for us to use our time, talents and treasure to build this world and to neglect the spiritual. This trap is avoided by investing in the work that holds eternal value, and not just temporal. What difference will it make in eternity? The fifth trap of Satan is to challenge our stand with contradiction and error. This trap is addressed with truth. We do not need to defend truth, but we do need to stand on it. Our stand is more important than our survival. Holding our position of faith in Jesus is essential.

Focus

Having addressed the discipline required in the spiritual conflict we now move to the requirement of focus, which is to keep our attention on the battle. Consider the oft repeated phrase, *The main thing is to keep the main thing, the main thing.* Many battles are lost simply because the resources have been sidetracked into other efforts. Focus is essential. If we are to aim at something, it must become the thing, the one thing, and the only thing. We are to be focused on the Lord Jesus and what He is doing rather than what Satan and his cohorts are doing. Dr. Henry Blackaby puts it this way, "Find out what the Lord is doing and join Him."

If we are to be victorious, we must fight the fight by faith. Or, to put it another way, we must not fight with our effort but trust the outcome to Jesus and do what He is directing. If you think about many of the battles in the Bible, men of God were asked to do things that, for lack of a better word, seemed crazy. Take Joshua marching around Jericho, for example. What about the boy, David fighting

Goliath the giant? Or what about Gideon facing a million-man army with a trumpet, a pitcher and a torch? Trust in the Lord is the order of the day, not self-glorying efforts.

Our focus is aided by keeping the goal of this battle clearly defined and at the forefront of our mind. Finishing what you start is very important to your sense of accomplishment, to your sense of direction and to your sense of importance. How you start is not near as important as how you finish. If you are to fight the fight of faith, you must keep your focus on Jesus, for Satan has a wealth of "good things to do" to move your focus from Jesus. This is one reason the battle with spiritual forces of darkness must be fought by faith in the Lord Jesus. He is never distracted and will keep us on course because we are trusting in Him and not in our own efforts. His victory has already been won, and though our participation won't change the outcome, it will expose the Lord as the only hope in this world when we follow Him by faith.

Skill

To win the battle also requires skill. I am not talking about ability or talents. That type of skill does not expose God for who He is but focuses on the individual and often hides God from view. The skill I am talking about is the skill that is acquired by experiences of faith.

> *For as many as are led by the Spirit of God, they are the sons of God.[131] But strong meat belongeth to them that are of full age, even those who by reason of use have their senses exercised to discern both good and evil.[132]*

God is not looking for great men but men of great faith. He does not need our fleshly efforts but can use every expression of faith in Him. Jesus taught that even a cup of cold water given "in His name" will be rewarded. The only way to increase your faith is to use the faith you have.

---

[131] Romans 8:4. In the original Greek, this verse reads "For as many as are continually being lead by the Spirit of God, they are the mature sons of God."

[132] Hebrews 5:14

Chapter 9

The Fight of Faith – The Fight Within

The first part of fighting by faith is the fight within. We will never grow up in faith until we learn to trust the Lord in our present situations.[133] Every time the flesh determines a course of action, the Spirit challenges it, and every time the Spirit determines a course of action, the flesh cries out in opposition. The flesh and the Spirit are in conflict and are struggling for different objectives. The Apostle Paul addresses this conflict in the seventh chapter of Romans when he says that the good that he intended to do or approve, he did not do it. But the evil, which he hated, he ended up doing. This is the real battle ground for the Christian. Paul concluded that he was a wretched man and that he needed a deliverer, for life in the flesh brings failure and death.

He addresses this conflict once again in the fifth chapter of Galatians. This time he references God's plan of deliverance, which is to walk in the Spirit, or to be led by the Spirit. He goes on to explain that the evidence of whether or not we are walking in the spirit is to look at our fruit. What are the results? Who is winning the battle? The results don't lie and whatever side you choose will produce fruit.

Jesus spoke of this conflict as well when He said a tree is known by its fruit.[134] We must choose which side we are on. Either we

---

[133] For the flesh lusteth against the Spirit, and the Spirit against the flesh: and these are contrary the one to the other: so that ye cannot do the things that ye would. Galatians 5:17

[134] Either make the tree good, and his fruit good; or else make the tree corrupt, and his fruit corrupt: for the tree is known by his fruit. Mt 12:33

stand for righteousness, or we stand on the flesh. There is no middle ground. This inner conflict is all about making this choice. We agonize over it because the nature of sin is like a drowning man fighting his rescuer. We want to be rescued, but we don't want to submit to what it takes to be rescued.

This conflict is one of the evidences that the Lord has begun His work in you. The unsaved do not face it. Their struggle is only to try hard, and then harder until they discover that it is an utter impossibility to overcome our lower nature by effort.

The conflict between the flesh and the Spirit is for dominance as to who will rule. Discipline is one of the tools we use to keep our old nature on the cross, but we will never defeat the old man until we kill him. Putting the old man to death is absolutely essential if we are to ever carry this battle to the enemy.[135] What we often do when the Lord allows us to face something that will mortally wound the old man is inadvertently nurse him back to health. We should never defend the carnal nature but rather accept the fact that he is totally depraved and only holds us back from becoming all that the Lord has planned for us to become.

Putting the old man to death requires cleansing and renewal. Sin must be confessed, for He will never fill an unclean vessel. To admit sin is not confession. Confession of sin is to see it as deadly and to take personal ownership of it. When this is done, it will produce a godly sorrow or contrition. That is what we bring to the Lord in our confession, just like Adam did when, confronted by God, he said "I was naked and I hid myself."[136] [137] To be forgiven does not mean that the sins did not happen but that the sins are now paid for and are no longer held against us. You may still remember them, but that does not mean that they are held against you. You must trust God in the forgiveness of them. A word of caution is needed here. Hebrews 5:13 says that, "For every one that useth milk is unskilful in the word of righteousness: for he is a babe." Do not try to skip dealing with your sin, thinking that it is not necessary. You must develop

---

[135] For he that is dead is freed from sin. Romans 6:7

[136] Genesis 3:10

[137] When we confess our sins, He is faithful (He will do it every time) and just (legally appropriate) to forgive us our sins, and to cleanse us from all unrighteousness. I john 1:9

your skill in walking by faith. You cannot trust your own feelings, for feelings are fickle and they change at the slightest opposition. You cannot trust your wisdom, for there are untold pitfalls that await the prideful. You cannot trust your own thinking, for it is limited and your knowledge is incomplete. You dare not trust another, for he has the same limitations and may not be as mature as you. The only thing that you dare trust is the Lord Himself. It will require everything of you. You need the seasoning of time and experiences in faith to mature. Once you have done a complete job of confession, you are a clean vessel, and you are prepared for renewal.

This renewal is what the Bible calls *being filled with the Holy Spirit*. This is not the same as receiving the Holy Spirit or being baptized in the Spirit, for that is accomplished at the moment of salvation and happens only once in the life of the believer.[138] On the other hand, the filling of the Holy Spirit happens multiple times in the life of the believer.[139] The word "filled" is the Greek word *pleroo* and means *to be controlled*. The purpose of the filling of the Holy Spirit is for service. The Lord will only use the believer when He (the Lord) is in control. This is also God's command, not an option. This is where the believer is to live. We know that we veer off course at times, and that is why He commands us to be filled repeatedly. When we veer off, we do not lose our salvation, but we do lose our fellowship and our witness. Without the filling of the Holy Spirit, we have no power to fight spiritually.

It is important to note that our fight is not with other humans. So many times we find ourselves thinking other people are out to get us. Satan would like us to fight each other, and then we fail to recognize it is he that is behind it all. The Bible teaches us that we are to love one another. It also teaches us that man was made in the similitude of God. It even teaches us to love our (human) enemies. The Devil is an instigator and causes all kinds of fights, and we erroneously believe that it was the person instead of the Devil behind it all. Is it no wonder we have such a struggle with faith in the Lord?

---

[138] One Lord, one faith, one baptism. Ephesians 4:5

[139] And be not drunk with wine, wherein is excess; but be filled with the Spirit. Ephesians 5:18

Where we are right now is where our faith can grow. Our present situation is exactly right to exercise our faith in the Lord. It doesn't matter if it is related to money, work, pressure, social problems, or health. The events of life are the opportunities for us to learn how to trust the Lord. Each lesson learned will move us on to greater faith opportunities. If you are facing great trials, you must exercise great faith in the Lord. This is God's chosen means of maturing in the faith. When faith in the Lord becomes the habit or chosen means of responding to life and its trials, we are ready then to take on any task or situation.

Chapter 10

The Fight of Faith – The Fight Without

Once we have fought the fight of faith within, we are now ready for the fight of faith without. Consider Ephesians 6:11-12:

Put on the whole armor of God, that ye may be able to stand against the wiles of the devil. 12 For we wrestle not against flesh and blood, but against principalities, against powers, against the rulers of the darkness of this world, against spiritual wickedness in high places.

First, notice that there is specific armor we are to use in this fight. Second, we are standing against the *tricks* or wiles of the devil. Finally, notice that the enemy is identified as spiritually degenerate angles whose leader is Satan.

Specific Armor

This armor is specifically addressed in *Eph 6:13-18:*

Wherefore take unto you the whole armor of God, that ye may be able to withstand in the evil day, and having done all, to stand. 14 Stand therefore, having your loins girt about with truth, and having on the breastplate of righteousness;

15 And your feet shod with the preparation of the gospel of peace; 16 Above all, taking the shield of faith, wherewith ye shall be able to quench all the fiery darts of the wicked. 17 And take the helmet of salvation, and the sword of the Spirit, which is the word of God: 18 Praying always with all prayer and supplication in the Spirit, and watching thereunto with all perseverance and supplication for all saints.

It is important to understand that our function is not to win or even survive. Our function is to stand. This is often difficult for people to accept, but it is nonetheless true. Consider that none of us will get out of this world alive (physically). The mortality rate for people is 100%. Therefore, it is not a question of if we will die, but what you will die for. Survival must be secondary to standing.

Winning cannot be our goal either because Christ has already defeated Satan. Our strengths are no match for Satan anyway, so entering into this conflict with the intention of winning with our strength would be futile. After all, the battle belongs to the Lord, not us. Our task in this conflict is to stand and properly represent Christ as a faith soldier, and trusting our protection to the Lord.

Our loins girded about with truth:

Once our purpose in spiritual conflict is established, we are now ready to get suited up in battle armor. It begins with having our loins girded about with truth, the only garment that we are to wear under the armor. There are no games to play and no outsmarting the enemy.

But above all things, my brethren, swear not, neither by heaven, neither by the earth, neither by any other oath: but let your yea be yea; and your nay, nay; lest ye fall into condemnation.[140]

Sometimes we feel that, if we speak the truth alone, we will embarrass ourselves. In reality, we will be embarrassed before the Lord, before all saints and even cause harm to the cause of Christ if we don't speak the truth and the truth alone. We do not need to

---

[140] James 5:12

shade the truth or protect the Lord in any way. He is quite capable of taking care of Himself. Honesty is demanded of those who are the representatives of our Lord. Dishonesty automatically disqualifies us to do spiritual battle, for it is basic in representing Christ. We must be honest to ourselves, our peers, our cause, our Lord and even our enemy. If we hold untruth, we will only frustrate the grace of our Lord and negate His power through us, in the conflict we are engaged in.

The breastplate of righteousness:

The second piece of armor we are to wear is the breastplate of righteousness. This piece of armor covers and protects vital organs of the body. It enables the arms and legs to function. One of the hardest things to break a Christian from is his belief in the merit system. He continues to try to please or impress the Lord. You often hear them reference deeds that they have or have not done. The truth is that we do not or cannot ever deserve anything from God but judgment. We should be thankful to God that we are on the Grace System and that it is not based on our worth, but His. What makes us righteous is nothing that we have or could earn. We are made righteous because of what Jesus did in paying for our sin,[141] so now there is nothing that can be brought against us because Jesus' payment is more than sufficient. Satan will attempt to stop your faith in the Lord by pointing out your failures. You must counter him by pointing out that your justification does not depend on your record but on that of Jesus. That is what gives you right standing, and you are acting on His record.

The gospel of peace:

The next piece of armor is the gospel of peace. The word gospel simply means good news. The good news is one of peace – the war is over. Satan was defeated at the cross, and Christ is already the victor. In order to understand this truth, we must understand the message today is one of life, how it became available, how it is to be lived, and many other teachings that are brought together in one book called the Bible. We are to study it and be directed by it. "All

---

[141] Here, righteous can also be understood as being in right standing with God.

scripture is given by inspiration of God, and is profitable for doctrine, for reproof, for correction, for instruction in righteousness."[142] Without knowing the Bible, we will not be equipped to fight in this conflict. The truth about who we are, why we are here, what power is available to us, who is really in charge and so many more things are found in it. What you believe is critical.

The shield of faith

The next piece of armor is the shield of faith. This entire book addresses the subject of faith, so I will not try to repeat what I have already written. Consider the purpose of the shield of faith, "that by it you may be able to quench the fiery darts of the devil."[143] This is an interesting phrase, as you would think that the purpose of a shield is to deflect the force rather than quench it. The fiery darts are in reference to a projectile that is not designed to kill as much as it is designed to inflict pain and to deter resistance. Satan's darts are aimed to pierce into you and set you on fire or burn you. They are also meant to create a sense of panic or desperation so that you would forfeit the fight to protect yourself. Notice, the shield of faith is to quench those darts, to extinguish them like water on a flame. Your confident dependence upon the Lord, or your faith in Him, does exactly that. It nullifies the effect of Satan's accusations and other efforts to defeat us. The more we know and trust the Lord, the less Satan has to fight us with. We are acting on His orders, and this is His fight.

The helmet of salvation:

The next piece of armor we are to put on is the helmet of salvation. The helmet protects the head, which is the command center of the body. Notice the reference is the *helmet of salvation*. We might also say that the helmet is the protector in the preservation of the individual. That protector is our Lord Jesus Christ. We will be confident while fighting because we are kept by the power of God. "Who are kept by the power of God through faith unto salvation ready to be revealed in the last time."[144] Our security is that the Lord is our

---

[142] 2 Timothy 3:16

[143] Ephesians 6:11

[144] 1 Peter 1:5

protection as well as our commander and redeemer. He redeemed us from our sin (salvation). He holds the outcome of the battle in His hand as the commander and chief (salvation), and he protects us in the conflict (salvation). He will preserve us through now and eternity.

The sword of the Spirit:

The sword of the Spirit is tied to the helmet of salvation as the natural product. We fight from a very secure position and therefore have boldness to obey the Spirit of God. The sword of the Spirit is identified as the Word of God, the Holy Bible, or the Scriptures. Now it is clarified that knowledge of the Scriptures is essential because it is the only offensive weapon the Christian has. Notice that the armor will protect the soldier doing battle but there is nothing to protect the back. This is because running away is not an option. The power of the scriptures to prick the heart or shut the mouth of the blasphemer cannot be overstated. The Lord will use his Word to stop the forces of darkness.

The armor of God closes with the admonition to pray. Multiple volumes have been written on prayer, so I will defer to the prayer giants that have treated this subject much better that I can; however, a few points are worth making. First, prayer is the means of communication in the spiritual realm. Prayer is not to change the mind of God but to change the mind of man. Also, prayer is to be made in full harmony with the Holy Spirit. It is to be continual (at all times) and in a state of urgency (alert with all perseverance). It is also to be a petition for all the saints, to watch out for the brethren.

The Tricks

The second thing to notice in this scripture is that Satan uses a variety of tricks such as deception, deceit, discouragement and denial. He would like us to believe this physical world is all there is to life. He would also like for us to believe that everything is dependent upon our own efforts. It is his desire for us to think that, if our good outweighs our bad, we will be okay. He deceives us into accepting that all there is to life is now and that there is nothing after we die. These and many more things that he perpetrates are lies. These things have partial truths at best but are deceptive and defeating. They are his tricks. What is true is that there is another world about us that is spiritual. There is the Lord Jesus who fights for those who trust in Him. Man's best effort is but an insult to what God has done to set us free from sin and death. There is an eternity to prepare for, as death is a portal not an end. When you know the truth, the truth shall set you free.[145] Before you will trust the Lord, you need to get to know Him. Only then you will trust Him.

This battle is expedited on the basis of principles not personalities. It is expedited spiritually rather than worldly, by truth rather than training, and through revelation rather than regulation. If you would effect change, you must establish a better way and convince the authorities to accept it. It begins by finding out where the Lord is working and joining Him. There are spiritual forces leading the authorities, and if they are stopped, the human forces will be easy. What we need to realize is that we are only a part of how God will address it. We must stand where and how He directs us.

There was a time when the Mississippi River was silting up at its entrance into the Gulf of Mexico and formed a delta that would not allow large shipping. To solve this problem, the local government imbedded large piers on each side of the river bed in a line that tapered from the main water course back to the bank, each one closer to the bank and further up the river. After all of the piers were set, branches were woven between the piers making a vertical mat that forced the water toward the main channel. The final effect was that the water was forced into the river channel, and because it was much narrower at the opening, the water flowed much faster and cleaned out the channel. In effect the river itself made the change in how it flowed.

We are not going to be able to control those in authority, but we can establish the principles and guidelines that will ultimately direct the natural flow of the use of that authority.

The enemy

Look again at the last part of Ephesians 6, verse 12. "For we wrestle not against flesh and blood, but against principalities, against powers, against the rulers of the darkness of this world,

---

[145] Ye shall know the truth, and the truth shall set you free. John 8:32

against spiritual wickedness in high places." This verse identifies the enemy. He is not flesh and blood but spirit. To understand the fight of faith, we need to take a look at what constitutes reality. There is a physical world that we understand through our 5 physical senses of sight, touch, smell, sound and taste. There is also a spiritual world coexisting with the physical world in which there are spiritual beings that are just as real as the physical beings but are not detected by the physical senses. This world is understood by the Word of God and through the revelation of the Holy Spirit. It is detected by our spiritual senses, and it affects the physical world. Reality is the sum of both the physical and spiritual worlds. The Lord Jesus Christ established it when he made the world and all that is in it.

> *Who is the image of the invisible God, the firstborn of every creature: 16 For by Him were all things created, that are in heaven, and that are in earth, visible and invisible, whether they be thrones, or dominions, or principalities, or powers: all things were created by Him, and for Him: 17 And He is before all things, and by Him all things consist.*[146]

The *Who/Him* is a reference to Jesus as the second person of the one triune God. He is what God looks like in the flesh. Note that He made all things, the visible and invisible, those that are in heaven and in earth. He also created all of the positions and beings for His own purpose. At the time of the creation, every being was in harmony with the Lord. It is important to recognize that, in the original creation, Lucifer and his subordinate angles were included as created beings and are therefore under His authority. The Bible describes when Lucifer rebelled against God:

> *How art thou fallen from heaven, O Lucifer, son of the morning! how art thou cut down to the ground, which didst weaken the nations! For thou hast said in thine heart, I will ascend into heaven, I will exalt my throne above the stars of God: I will sit also upon the mount of the congregation, in the sides of the north: I will ascend above the heights of*

---

[146] Colossians 1:15-18

the clouds; I will be like the most High. Yet thou shalt be brought down to hell, to the sides of the pit; there was a war in heaven and he and a third of the angles were cast out of heaven.[147]

And there was war in heaven: Michael and his angels fought against the dragon; and the dragon fought and his angels[148]

It is understood by most Biblical scholars that Lucifer is Satan and is know by many names[149] and the fallen angels are understood to be demons and are a part of Satan's kingdom[150] and do his bidding. Satan's kingdom is in contrast to the kingdom of God. It is a kingdom of darkness, whereas God's kingdom is of light. Satan's kingdom is one of death, but God's kingdom is one of life. In Ephesians 6:12, you have a description of Satan's kingdom of darkness with which we are to fight against by faith. His domain is in this world, extends into the physical and spiritual arenas and includes both the seen and unseen. This is not an imaginary kingdom but is very real. His control reaches into seats of principalities, powers, dominion and authority. Jesus exposed the Jews and Pharisees as being under Satan's control

Ye are of your father the devil, and the lusts of your father ye will do. He was a murderer from the beginning, and abode not in the truth, because there is no truth in him. When he speaketh a lie, he speaketh of his own: for he is a liar, and the father of it.[151]

Satan would have us think that he isn't real and is just a myth. He would also like for us to think that these rulers of darkness are harmless in the same way that they are presented in movies and on TV. He would like for us to think there is no demon possession today and that we have outgrown such nonsense. These forces of darkness

---

[147] Isaiah 15:13-14

[148] Revelation 12:7

[149] See Appendix 10.1

[150] See Appendix 10.2

[151] John 8:44

are Satan and his demons, or fallen angles. Satan's army is quite sophisticated and is equipped with spiritual power. The demons seek to control individuals and cause them to do unthinkable acts. They will offer whatever treasures of the world are required to seduce their followers and simply collect it back again upon their death. They have no conscience, sense of morality or guilt. They are insidious and relentless. They hate the Lord Jesus and Christians. They are opposed to all that is right and will stoop to any level to oppose it. They are neither moral nor reasonable. They are not trustworthy. They are base, their desires are twisted, and they take pleasure in inflicting pain and suffering. They are evil in their hearts and merciless in their practice. Their conscience is seared, and they do not feel guilt.

As a result of Adam's original sin, all people of all nations, races and time begin life with a fallen nature. Until this sin nature has been replaced with a new nature,[152] all are children of the Devil. As such, they are prime candidates to enlist in Satan's army. When enlisted, they become the minions of Satan and are servants of darkness and worship Satan. They may carry such titles as witches, mediums, spiritualist, warlock, wizard sorcerer and the like. They also seek to work in places of authority to affect their control over man. These individuals are not normal humans. They have come under the control of Satan and follow his ways. In some cases, they are even possessed by demonic spirits. They have given themselves over to darkness and delight in tearing down the establishment. They are supported by the powers of darkness and in full partnership with it.[153]

As mentioned in chapter 3, there are seven authority structures that the Lord has established in this world for the purposes of our learning how to rule, for the benefit of mankind and for our protection against misuse of authority. In this context we are addressing the misuse of authority. This misuse could be in the area of personal profit, personal pleasure or personal control over others for a variety of wrong reasons. The 7 authorities that were established by God are:

---

[152] A new nature is the result of a spiritual birth by believing in Jesus.

[153] See Appendix 10.3

Marital Authority	Husband/Wife
Parental Authority	Parents/Children
Educational Authority	Teacher/Student
Administrative Authority	Employer/Employee
Governmental Authority	Government/Citizen
Ecclesiastical Authority	Church/Member
Scriptural Authority	Bible/Person

Each of these authorities was established for the purpose of benefit for the whole of mankind. When exercised properly, they are indeed a blessing, but when they are misused, they become a curse to those affected by them. Whenever you stand in the way of God's intended plan, you are fighting God, and the consequences are devastating. It is important to point out that, at its heart, every sin has a rejection of the authority God has established. [154] If we are going to walk by faith in the Lord, we must do what He says in His word.

These seven authorities work together like an umbrella to shield us from the devastation of sin. When any one or any combination of these is compromised, we are exposed to sin's devastation. That is why we have people suffering from hunger and disease and tragedies and brutality. It is not because God doesn't care or because He is uninvolved. It is because there is sin in the camp, and innocent people suffer from it. If we would deal with the sin within, we would see blessings follow. It is not so much that God allows it as much as we allow it. When we obey the Lord, it opens the way for the Lord to work on our behalf. When we hold to our sin, we shut the door to God's power and open the door to Satan. It is essential to fight the fight of faith in order to shut the door on Satan and open it to the Lord. Believing the revelation of the Lord is so important because sin-sized problems can only be solved by God-sized solutions. Where are these warriors who will stand in the gaps and fight the

---

[154] Whosoever therefore resisteth the power resisteth the ordinance of God: and they that resist shall receive to themselves damnation. Romans 13:2 But he giveth more grace. Wherefore he saith, God resisteth the proud, but giveth grace unto the humble. James 4:6 Likewise, ye younger, submit yourselves unto the elder. Yea, all of you be subject one to another, and be clothed with humility: for God resisteth the proud, and giveth grace to the humble. 1Peter 5:5

fight of faith against the misuse of authority so our homes will be safe, our marriages will stand, our educators will teach truth, our employers will be fair, our politicians will serve the masses and our pastors and church leadership will be spiritual and maintain a spiritual leadership? Only the Lord can raise great men of faith so that we will see sin's devastation turned back.

Chapter 11

The Victory of Faith

*For whatsoever is born of God, overcometh the world; and
this is the victory that overcometh the world, even our faith.*
                                                    – I John 5:4

Victory means different things to different people, but within
the context of this verse, it is tied specifically to the idea of
overcoming the world or world system. The main objective of the
Lord is to free us from the hold that this world has on us.

Nikao is the Greek word for "overcometh" and literally means
"hath overcome and continues to overcome." In other words, this
victory is not one success, but one of continual success. It is a pattern
of life lived in the attitude of faith in the Lord Jesus. This victory is
one that is already accomplished. Christ already overcame the world
through His death on the cross. In John 16:33, the Savior says, "Be
of good cheer; I have overcome the world." Therefore, it is not our
job to overcome the world. Our job is to believe in Christ, who has
already overcome the world. We will always be disappointed in our
attempts to overcome the world, but we will never be disappointed
in the work that Christ has already done.

And what of this world is there to overcome? The apostle John
described it in I John 2:16. "For all that is in the world; the lust
of the flesh, the lust of the eyes and the pride of life is not of the
Father but of the world." I heard a preacher describe it as, "Passions,
Possessions and Positions."

The *lust of the flesh* is the appetites and cravings of the body that are out of control. It is our focus on fleshly desires. It is the things that demand sensational feelings and emotions. It is the root of addiction and the basis of dissatisfaction. The *lust of the eyes* refers to the things that you can possess. It is the material possessions that you are seeking to control. It is the "I own" of your heart and exposes your obsession to have more. The *pride of life* is the opinion of superiority that we hold of ourselves. It is manifested in the desire to control or be in charge of everything. What cannot be controlled is of no value, should be destroyed and exposes our sin of rebellion.

This carnality is the state of sin that we are born in and how we live our lives until we are born again, at which time there is a new man created, one that is new and different from the former, or natural man. The natural man is worldly and will always choose the world.[155] He is always fighting for control of the New Nature (spiritual man). The new nature is spiritual and is eternal. II Corinthians 5:17 says that "If any man be in Christ, he is a new creation of God. Old things are passed away, behold all things are become new." The new nature is dominated and directed by God's Holy Spirit that we receive when we are born again. We are exhorted to put off the old man[156] and to put on the new man.[157]

The old man is the bitter enemy of the new man and must be cast off. Young Christians often miss this truth. The question of just how to handle the old man arises once we determine to cast the old man off. We begin lightly by trying to reason with him, but he is unreasonable. We try to control him, but he will not obey. We try to reform him, but he will not be changed. We try to bargain with him, but he will not keep any agreement. We try to force him, but he is very strong. When he is wounded, he raises such a cry and fuss that we soon give in to nurse him back to health. We try to isolate him, but he calls in reinforcements. It is the nature of the old man to sin, and he will always sin when given the chance. Jeremiah says that "the heart is deceitful and desperately wicked, and who

---

[155] Carnality is the predominance of thought and practice inclined toward the world system of Passions, Possessions and Positions.

[156] Ephesians 4:22

[157] Ephesians 2:23

can know it?" The depth of depravity of the natural man is seen in Romans 3:23: "All have sinned and come short of the glory of God." In Isaiah 53:6 "All we like sheep have gone astray; we have turned everyone to his own way." Also, in Romans 3:12: "They are all gone out of the way, they are together become unprofitable; there is none that doeth good, no, not one."

It is difficult to convince a person that the old man or his carnal nature is totally depraved. We may acknowledge that there is sin, but we argue that there is more good than bad in us. We then are given a better look at ourselves and conclude that there is more sin than we expected but that there is still a lot of good. As we continue to discover our true nature, we bargain with God acknowledging that yes there is a lot of sin, but there is still some good. It is not until we finally face the fact that the old man is totally depraved and unredeemable that we conclude there is no victory with him.

The old man is totally depraved and must be killed, but this leads us to the question of just how we can accomplish this.

Knowing this that our old man is crucified with Him, that the body of sin might be destroyed, that hence forth you might not serve sin. For he that is dead is freed from sin. [158]

I am crucified with Christ: nevertheless I live; yet not I, but Christ liveth in me: and the life which I now live in the flesh I live by the faith of the Son of God, who loved me, and gave himself for me. [159]

It begins with the statement that, as a believer, I am crucified with Christ. Immediately we want to draw back. It was one thing for Jesus to die on a cross, but I don't want to. That is the flesh crying out against the work of God. It is often stated that Christians have been crucified with Christ. We don't go through the physical crucifixion, but we are on his cross just the same. The purpose of crucifixion was death, and that is what we are facing. This is how the old man is dealt with. As he dies, the believer discovers the next

---

[158] Romans 6:6-7

[159] Galatians 2:20

part of the above verse, which is, "nevertheless I live." This is the life that Jesus referenced when He declared, "I am come that ye may have life," and again, "I am the life." In reality, it is the life of Christ that we are living. Life for the believer then consists of living by faith in Jesus, trusting and relying on Him and His Word.

It is important to clarify that I am not suggesting that we are to commit physical suicide. Here, scripture is referring to the nature we hold in our heart to maintain control of our lives verses living by faith in Jesus as Lord of life. The problem is in our heart, not our bodies. No amount of physical suffering can change the heart. Though we are wounded or even die physically, the heart will remain unchanged without the working of the Holy Spirit on the individual. The old man holds the belief in his heart that self-government is the way to live. Therefore, it is the attitude of self-reliance and self-direction that must die. As II Corinthians 5:17 stated, *"Old things are passed away."* Failure to properly deal with this issue will block our victory in the spiritual life. We must aggressively and persistently attack this old lifestyle and put to death the possibility of even trying to live our life without faith in Jesus as our Lord.

How then is the old man to die? Crucifixion was a horrible death and was intended to inflict as much pain as possible. Jesus endured that pain for us so that we do not have to suffer through it. Even so, it still affects the believer. Crucifixion was so certain that an individual's death was recorded at the moment the nails were driven, even though his actual death may not come for hours or even days later. So it is with the old man. Our crucifixion is complete when we become a believer. The death of the old man is so certain that it is referenced as a completed act, even though we still have the old nature.[160]

It is also important to point out the process of writhing during the time of hanging on the cross. Little is said today about the process, but there is something important for us to learn here. The process of writhing involved the full weight of an individual's body hanging on nails that were driven through the base of the hand and feet, where many nerve ending cross. Paralysis would begin in the arms and would follow down to the chest, which would prevent the individual

---

[160] Galatians 2:20

from taking a breath. In order to breathe, the crucified would push down on the nail in his feet and use his shoulder blades to walk up the rough cross. This would relieve the pressure on the hands and arms but would last only until the legs would give out. The body would slump down again, putting pressure back on the pierced hands. The process would begin again until there was no more strength to make another push up the cross and suffocation would finally kill the individual. This process describes what many Christians go through fighting with the flesh—writhing up and down on the cross, resisting death to the old man. When Jesus was crucified, we find that He died fairly quickly because He yielded to the death of the cross. We can shorten the trial by yielding to a sure outcome. When the old man is insulted, don't defend him. When his character is attacked, agree. If he is wounded, don't nurse him back to health. It is the Lord's responsibility to justify the believer. It is the responsibility of the believer to trust the Lord with his life and his work.

Let us now look at the victory that is ours by placing our faith in the Lord. First, the power of sin over us was broken when Jesus died on the cross. Satan lost all power over the believer because Jesus has justified him.[161] Satan cannot force the believer to sin against his will, for he has no power over him. Not only has Satan lost any power he may have had over the believer, but the believer has been given whatever power is needed to be conformed to the image of Christ.[162] At this point, the Spirit of the believer is completed in the image of the Lord.

Not only was the power of sin broken but the persuasion of sin is broken as we walk in faith in the Lord. We are focused on the Lord, His word and His will. This is a process called *Sanctification* or *setting apart*. From the moment a person first places their faith in Jesus as Lord of their life until the time of his death (or rapture), the will and spirit of the believer undergo restructuring. We learn through our study, experience and surrender to the Lord that God was right about everything. We change our mind about the world and adopt

---

[161] There is therefore now no condemnation to them which are in Christ Jesus, who walk not after the flesh, but after the Spirit. Romans 8:1

[162] But as many as received Him, to them gave He power to become the sons of God. John 1:12

the ways and thoughts of the Lord. It doesn't matter how many times we fail to walk in faith along the way. This is a process, not a race. The goal is that we be conformed to the image of the Lord and not to string together a list of successes. It is more important that we trust Him because we are His main project.[163] It is His responsibility to deliver us completed, and it is His skill that will shape us, not ours.

One day the Lord will return in the air to catch us away (often referred to as the rapture), and we will be changed.[164] Our new body will be like that of the Lord's resurrected body. Sin will have no place in it, and the presence of sin will be separated from our members.[165] Then our victory over Satan, sin and self will be complete.

There is an epilogue to this victory of faith. When we are caught away with the Lord, we will go to the Bema judgment. When we hear the word "judgment," we often think of it as a harsh, strict punishment. But take note of this application. The believer's sin was judged in Christ at the cross, so all of the negative connotations are completed and finished. What is left? Rewards are all that is left, my friend. The Bema Judgment is an award ceremony. Every act of faith in the Lord will be recognized and awarded. All failure and sin has already been judged at the cross. It is not something to be feared but something to be anticipated. The awards are for the Lord, for what He has done with us. He will hold us up that all may behold what we have become by trusting Him. Now His intended plan for us[166] will be complete, and we will forever reflect His image.

The Bible speaks often about faith and for a great reason. Faith is the only way to please God, and whatsoever is not of faith is sin. Faith is the only reasonable and acceptable way to live. We must

---

[163] For we are his workmanship, created in Christ Jesus unto good works, which God hath before ordained that we should walk in them. Ephesians 2:10

[164] Behold, I shew you a mystery; We shall not all sleep, but we shall all be changed, In a moment, in the twinkling of an eye, at the last trump: for the trumpet shall sound, and the dead shall be raised incorruptible, and we shall be changed. 1Corinthians 15:51-52

[165] And the very God of peace sanctify you wholly; and I pray God your whole spirit and soul and body be preserved blameless unto the coming of our Lord Jesus Christ. I Thessalonians 5:23

[166] And God said, Let us make man in our image, after our likeness: and let them have dominion over the fish of the sea, and over the fowl of the air, and over the cattle, and over all the earth, and over every creeping thing that creepeth upon the earth. Genesis 1:26

learn to live by faith here because that is how we will live in heaven. If you don't establish it here, what awaits you there? It is my prayer that you will not only become proficient in walking by faith but that you will excel in your faith in the Lord Jesus.

Appendix

5.1

You may want to study through the following Scriptures to gain some additional insight on this subject of obedience:

Ro 1:5 By whom we have received grace and apostleship, for obedience to the faith among all nations, for His name:

Ro 5:19 For as by one man's disobedience many were made sinners, so by the obedience of One shall many be made righteous.

Ro 6:16 Know ye not, that to whom ye yield yourselves servants to obey, his servants ye are to whom ye obey; whether of sin unto death, or of obedience unto righteousness?

Ro 16:19 For your obedience is come abroad unto all men. I am glad therefore on your behalf: but yet I would have you wise unto that which is good, and simple concerning evil.

Ro 16:26 But now is made manifest, and by the scriptures of the prophets, according to the commandment of the everlasting God, made known to all nations for the obedience of faith:

1Co 14:34 Let your women keep silence in the churches: for it is not permitted unto them to speak; but they are commanded to be under obedience, as also saith the law.

2Co 7:15 And his inward affection is more abundant toward you, whilst He remembereth the obedience of you all, how with fear and trembling ye received Him.

2Co 10:5 Casting down imaginations, and every high thing that exalteth itself against the knowledge of God, and bringing into captivity every thought to the obedience of Christ;

2Co 10:6 And having in a readiness to revenge all disobedience, when your obedience is fulfilled.

Phm 1:21 Having confidence in thy obedience I wrote unto thee, knowing that thou wilt also do more than I say.

Heb 5:8 Though he were a Son, yet learned He obedience by the things which He suffered;

1Pe 1:2 Elect according to the foreknowledge of God the Father, through sanctification of the Spirit, unto obedience and sprinkling of the blood of Jesus Christ: Grace unto you, and peace, be multiplied.

Ro 2:8 But unto them that are contentious, and do not obey the truth, but obey unrighteousness, indignation and wrath,

Ro 6:12 Let not sin therefore reign in your mortal body, that ye should obey it in the lusts thereof.

Ga 3:1 O foolish Galatians, who hath bewitched you, that ye should not obey the truth, before whose eyes Jesus Christ hath been evidently set forth, crucified among you?

Ga 5:7 Ye did run well; who did hinder you that ye should not obey the truth? {hinder you: or, drive you back}

Eph 6:1 Children, obey your parents in the Lord: for this is right.

Col 3:20 Children, obey your parents in all things: for this is well pleasing unto the Lord.

Col 3:22 Servants, obey in all things your masters according to the flesh; not with eyeservice, as menpleasers; but in singleness of heart, fearing God:

2Th 1:8 In flaming fire taking vengeance on them that know not God, and that obey not the gospel of our Lord Jesus Christ: {taking: or, yielding}

2Th 3:14 And if any man obey not our word by this epistle, note that man, and have no company with him, that he may be ashamed. {by...: or, signify that man by an epistle}

Tit 3:1 Put them in mind to be subject to principalities and powers, to obey magistrates, to be ready to every good work,

Heb 5:9 And being made perfect, He became the author of eternal salvation unto all them that obey Him;

Heb 13:17 Obey them that have the rule over you, and submit yourselves: for they watch for your souls, as they that must give account, that they may do it with joy, and not with grief: for that is unprofitable for you. {have...: or, guide}

Jas 3:3 Behold, we put bits in the horses' mouths, that they may obey us; and we turn about their whole body.

1Pe 3:1 Likewise, ye wives, be in subjection to your own husbands; that, if any obey not the word, they also may without the word be won by the conversation of the wives;

1Pe 4:17 For the time is come that judgment must begin at the house of God: and if it first begin at us, what shall the end be of them that obey not the gospel of God?

5.2

Look at a few of the promises the Lord gave us, considering only the gospel of John.

Jn 1:12 But as many as received Him, to them gave He power to become the sons of God, even to them that believe on His name:

Jn 3:16 For God so loved the world, that He gave His only begotten Son, that whosoever believeth in Him should not perish, but have everlasting life.

John 7:38 He that believeth on Me, as the scripture hath said, out of his belly shall flow rivers of living water.

John 8:12 Then spake Jesus again unto them, saying, I am the light of the world: he that followeth Me shall not walk in darkness, but shall have the light of life.

John 8:32 And ye shall know the truth, and the truth shall make you free.

John 8:36 If the Son therefore shall make you free, ye shall be free indeed.

John 8:51 Verily, verily, I say unto you, If a man keep My saying, he shall never see death.

John 11:26 And whosoever liveth and believeth in Me shall never die. Believest thou this?

John 13:17 If ye know these things, happy are ye if ye do them.

John 14:21 He that hath my commandments, and keepeth them, he it is that loveth Me: and he that loveth Me shall be loved of my Father, and I will love him, and will manifest Myself to him.

John 15:5 I am the vine, ye are the branches: He that abideth in Me, and I in him, the same bringeth forth much fruit: for without M ye can do nothing.

John 15:7 If ye abide in Me, and My words abide in you, ye shall ask what ye will, and it shall be done unto you.

John 15:16 Ye have not chosen Me, but I have chosen you, and ordained you, that ye should go and bring forth fruit, and that your fruit should remain: that whatsoever ye shall ask of the Father in My name, He may give it you.

6.1

Mt 7:7 Ask, and it shall be given you; seek, and ye shall find; knock, and it shall be opened unto you: 8 For every one that asketh receiveth; and he that seeketh findeth; and to him that knocketh it shall be opened.

Mt 18:19 Again I say unto you, That if two of you shall agree on earth as touching any thing that they shall ask, it shall be done for them of my Father which is in heaven.

Mt 19:26 But Jesus beheld them, and said unto them, With men this is impossible; but with God all things are possible.

Mt 21:21 Jesus answered and said unto them, Verily I say unto you, If ye have faith, and doubt not, ye shall not only do this which is done to the fig tree, but also if ye shall say unto this mountain, Be thou removed, and be thou cast into the sea; it shall be done.

Mt 22 And all things, whatsoever ye shall ask in prayer, believing, ye shall receive.

Mt 28:18 And Jesus came and spake unto them, saying, All power is given unto me in heaven and in earth.

19 Go ye therefore, and teach all nations, baptizing them in the name of the Father, and of the Son, and of the Holy Ghost: {teach...: or, make disciples, or, Christians of all nations}

20 Teaching them to observe all things whatsoever I have commanded you: and, lo, I am with you alway, even unto the end of the world.

Mr 10:27 And Jesus looking upon them saith, With men it is impossible, but not with God: for with God all things are possible.

Lu 11:8 I say unto you, Though he will not rise and give him, because he is his friend, yet because of his importunity he will rise and give him as many as he needeth.

Lu 11:9 And I say unto you, Ask, and it shall be given you; seek, and ye shall find; knock, and it shall be opened unto you.

Lu 11:10 For every one that asketh receiveth; and he that seeketh findeth; and to him that knocketh it shall be opened.

Lu 11:11 If a son shall ask bread of any of you that is a father, will he give him a stone? or if he ask a fish, will he for a fish give him a serpent?

Lu 11:12 Or if he shall ask an egg, will he offer him a scorpion? {offer: Gr. give}

Lu 11:13 If ye then, being evil, know how to give good gifts unto your children: how much more shall your heavenly Father give the Holy Spirit to them that ask him?

Lu 18:27 And he said, The things which are impossible with men are possible with God.

Lu 24:49 And, behold, I send the promise of my Father upon you: but tarry ye in the city of Jerusalem, until ye be endued with power from on high.

Joh 1:12 But as many as received him, to them gave he power to become the sons of God, even to them that believe on his name:

Joh 14:13 And whatsoever ye shall ask in my name, that will I do, that the Father may be glorified in the Son.

Joh 14:14 If ye shall ask any thing in my name, I will do it.

Joh 15:7 If ye abide in me, and my words abide in you, ye shall ask what ye will, and it shall be done unto you.

Joh 15:16 Ye have not chosen me, but I have chosen you, and ordained you, that ye should go and bring forth fruit, and that your fruit should remain: that whatsoever ye shall ask of the Father in my name, he may give it you.

Joh 16:23 And in that day ye shall ask me nothing. Verily, verily, I say unto you, Whatsoever ye shall ask the Father in my name, he will give it you.

Joh 16:26 At that day ye shall ask in my name: and I say not unto you, that I will pray the Father for you:

Ac 1:8 But ye shall receive power, after that the Holy Ghost is come upon you: and ye shall be witnesses unto me both in Jerusalem, and in all Judaea, and in Samaria, and unto the uttermost part of the earth.

Ro 8:11 But if the Spirit of him that raised up Jesus from the dead dwell in you, he that raised up Christ from the dead shall also quicken your mortal bodies by his Spirit that dwelleth in you.

1Co 2:4 And my speech and my preaching was not with enticing words of man's wisdom, but in demonstration of the Spirit and of power:

1Co 2:9 But as it is written, Eye hath not seen, nor ear heard, neither have entered into the heart of man, the things which God hath prepared for them that love him.

Eph 1:19 And what is the exceeding greatness of his power to us-ward who believe, according to the working of his mighty power,

Eph 3:20 Now unto him that is able to do exceeding abundantly above all that we ask or think, according to the power that worketh in us,

Eph 6:10 Finally, my brethren, be strong in the Lord, and in the power of his might.

Php 3:10 That I may know him, and the power of his resurrection, and the fellowship of his sufferings, being made conformable unto his death;

Jas 1:5 If any of you lack wisdom, let him ask of God, that giveth to all men liberally, and upbraideth not; and it shall be given him.

Jas 1:6 But let him ask in faith, nothing wavering. For he that wavereth is like a wave of the sea driven with the wind and tossed.

Jas 4:2 Ye lust, and have not: ye kill, and desire to have, and cannot obtain: ye fight and war, yet ye have not, because ye ask not.

Jas 4:3 Ye ask, and receive not, because ye ask amiss, that ye may consume it upon your lusts.

1Jo 3:22 And whatsoever we ask, we receive of him, because we keep his commandments, and do those things that are pleasing in his sight.

1Jo 5:14 And this is the confidence that we have in him, that, if we ask any thing according to his will, he heareth us: {in: or, concerning}

1Jo 5:15 And if we know that he hear us, whatsoever we ask, we know that we have the petitions that we desired of him.

Re 2:26 And he that overcometh, and keepeth my works unto the end, to him will I give power over the nations:

Re 11:3 And I will give power unto my two witnesses, and they shall prophesy a thousand two hundred and threescore days, clothed in sackcloth.

Re 11:6 These have power to shut heaven, that it rain not in the days of their prophecy: and have power over waters to turn them to blood, and to smite the earth with all plagues, as often as they will.

Re 20:6 Blessed and holy is he that hath part in the first resurrection: on such the second death hath no power, but they shall be priests of God and of Christ, and shall reign with him a thousand years.

8.1

Repentance of sin. Notice that Jesus died for the sin (singular) of the world. It was not the sins (plural) that we commit that create the division between God and Man, but THE SIN. The sins (acts that are sinful) are the product of this sin that is resident and president of the heart. This sin is the heart of man that rejects the authority of God on man and refuses to follow Him. It is the exact opposite of faith in God. Making yourself the authority and living according to the fallen nature of man is the problem. This must be corrected for the fellowship to be restored to its intended purpose.

8.2

Faith in Jesus as Lord of Life.

Faith is reliance upon or trust. This faith is placed in Jesus and no longer in yourself. In order to trust Jesus, there must be a distrust of self government. So long as there is no surrender of this control, there is no faith in Jesus and consequently, no salvation. The fleshly self (old man) must be dethroned and put out of business because he is sold out to this world and its ways. Only when the Lord is in control does eternal change take place and new life begins. Salvation is not a religious experience but a relationship whereas He not only takes charge; He also takes responsibility for the individual. He removes the consequence of death from the believer who is indwelled with the Hold Spirit who is charged with comforting, leading, teaching and training the new believer.

10.1
Titles and Names of the Devil. Willmington, H.L.: Willmington's Book of Bible Lists. Wheaton, IL : Tyndale, 1987, S. 303

1.   Abaddon. Re 9:11.
2.   Accuser of our brethren. Re 12:10.
3.   Adversary. 1Pe 5:8.
4.   Angel of the bottomless pit. Re 9:11.
5.   Apollyon. Re 9:11.
6.   Beelzebub. Mt 12:24.
7.   Belial. 2Co 6:15.
8.   Crooked serpent. Isa 27:1.
9.   Dragon. Isa 27:1; Re 20:2.
10. Enemy. Mt 13:39.
11. Evil spirit. 1Sa 16:14.
12. Father of lies. Joh 8:44.
13. Great red dragon. Re 12:3.
14. Leviathan. Isa 27:1.
15. Liar. Joh 8:44.
16. Lying spirit. 1Ki 22:22.
17. Murderer. Joh 8:44.
18. Old serpent. Re 12:9; 20:2.
19. Piercing serpent. Isa 27:1.
20. Power of darkness. Col 1:13.
21. Prince of this world. Joh 14:30.
22. Prince of the devils. Mt 12:24.
23. Prince of the power of the air. Eph 2:2.

Ref 10.2
20 facts about fallen angles Willmington, H.L.: Willmington's Book of Bible Lists. Wheaton, IL : Tyndale, 1987, S. 304

1. Fallen angels have names.	Luke 8:30; Rev. 9:11
2. They speak.	Luke 4:34, 41; 8:28; Matt. 8:29; Mark 5:12; Acts 19:15; Mark 3:11
3. They know who Jesus is.	Luke 4:34
4. They know of future damnation.	Matt. 8:29
5. They know the saved from the unsaved.	Rev. 9:4
6. They are able to formulate a Satan-centered systematic theology.	1 Tim. 4:1
7. They possess great strength.	Exod. 8:7; 7:11-12; Dan. 10:13; Mark 5:2-4; 9:17-26; Acts 19:16; 2 Cor. 10:4-5; Rev. 9:15-19
8. They experience fear.	Luke 8:28; James 2:19
9. They display disdain.	Acts 16:15
10. There are unchained angels, having a certain amount of freedom at the present time.	Ps. 78:49; Eph. 6:12; Rev. 12:7-9
11. There are chained angels, having no freedom at the present time.	2 Pet. 2:4
12. There are evil angels who rule over the nations of this world.	Dan. 10:13
13. A wicked angel named Legion headed up a large group of fallen spirits that had possessed the maniac of Gadara.	Mark 5:9
14. The bottomless pit is under the control of an angel called Abaddon (in the Hebrew) and Apollyon (in the Greek).	Rev. 9:11

10.3

Barnes notes has this commentary on the extent of Satan's kingdom in the physical world. Barnes Notes: on rulers of darkness of this world. "It is a warfare on a large scale with the entire kingdom of darkness over the world. Yet, in maintaining the warfare, the struggle will be with such portions of that kingdom as we come in contact with, and will actually relate

(1.) to our own sinful propensities—which are a part of the kingdom of darkness;

(2.) with the evil passions of others—their pride, ambition, and spirit of revenge—which are also a part of that kingdom;

(3) with the evil customs, laws, opinions, employments, pleasures of the world—which are also a part of that dark kingdom;

(4) with error, superstition, false doctrine—which are also a part of that kingdom; and

(5) with the wickedness of the heathen world—the sins of benighted nations —-also a part of that kingdom. Wherever we come in contact with evil—whether in our own hearts or elsewhere— there we are to make war. "

About the Author: Vernon Ball

Balancing a spiritual life with secular work is nothing new to Pastor Ball. It is something that has been routine for the more than 44 years he has been in the ministry. During that time, he served smaller churches that could not fully support him and his family, and he was required to hold down a secular job to care for them. As a bi-vocational pastor, two full time jobs (pastoring and secular) was the norm. In addition to a bi-vocational ministry, he and his wife, Darla raised seven children. They now have 21 grandchildren and 4 great grandchildren. Not too many will find a greater demand on their time.

Pastor Ball is a graduate of Clear Creek Baptist College in Pineville, KY. He has pastored five churches, three in Colorado, one in Kentucky and one in Maryland. In addition, he has served as Interim Pastor for 5 additional churches, Educational Director for 11 years, served for nearly 2 years as a home missionary, has taken two mission trips to the Sioux Indian Reservation in North Dakota, started a mission in Colorado, preached revivals, pulpit supply, led a week-long retreat for young ministers, was a speaker for a financial money management conference, participated in rest home and jail ministries and mentored multiple preachers and special service workers from his churches.

God has blessed his secular work, which was also one of responsibility. At 18, he managed his father's produce business. He was on a survey crew for the State of Colorado at 19. He later worked on highway construction and ran some of the heavy equipment. He worked for Pacific Bell for over a year and was recognized by its

CEO for outstanding work. He worked in the Molybdenum mines in Colorado as a miner and was asked to join the engineers, where he worked for over four years. He began working in building construction as a laborer and was promoted to carpenter apprentice, then journeyman carpenter, then labor foreman, and crane operator, all within one year. He holds the philosophy that it is just as spiritual to serve the Lord in your labor as it is in your worship. He credits the Lord and the one who has given him success by following these verses:

> *Whether therefore ye eat, or drink, or whatsoever ye do, do all to the glory of God.*
> —1 Colossians 10:31

> *And whatsoever ye do in word or deed, do all in the name of the Lord Jesus, giving thanks to God and the Father by him.*
> — Colossians 3:17

> *And whatsoever ye do, do it heartily, as to the Lord, and not unto men.*
> — Colossians 3:23

It has been a burning desire in his heart from early in his ministry to equip the saints to do the work of ministering. He has been in the trenches with the common man and worked as the leader. He has shared the workload of the laborer and prayed with the overburdened. One of the great concerns he has is that the average Christian is not enjoying the *normal* Christian life. The Bible teaches that we are to be overcomers of this world, yet all too often the Christian is tossed to and fro with every wind of doctrine. The doctrine of faith is one of the basic doctrines in which there is so much confusion. It is his desire that this book will help the believer to clarify what he believes and who he is trusting so that his faith in the Lord will enable him to stand against the tricks of the devil.

> *I have no greater joy than to hear of my children walking in truth.*
> — III John 4

CPSIA information can be obtained at www.ICGtesting.com
Printed in the USA
BVOW020019050613

322431BV00007B/18/P